The Civilian Guide to Leading Your Troops

By

DAVID CIARELLA

DEDICATION

This book is humbly dedicated to all those men and women I have served under. The good ones, you may know who you are, especially Colonel Louis Hightower and Jim Ajello. Colonel, you helped a young lieutenant to gain confidence in decision making and Jim, you showed me how to have trust and faith in your team members. And to those leaders who probably weren't so good? Well, thank you, I learned from you, too.

TABLE OF CONTENTS

INTRODUCTION

Like many people in corporate America, I think that there is a big void when it comes to real leadership. While there are examples of good leadership from time to time, you just don't encounter many people who brag about what a great leader they have for a boss. Many people say, "I have a great boss," which often implies leniency or someone who is approachable and easy to talk with. When is the last time you heard someone say, "My boss is a great leader"? Probably not lately.

And why is that? Why can't corporate America seem to turn out great leaders anymore? Why do there seem to be so many sycophants, so many uninspiring desk jockeys, so much office politics, improper and unethical behavior, and so many managers afraid to confront and deal honestly with problems?

I think the partial answer is that we reward those types of behaviors and encourage too many potential leaders to be exactly like that. In addition, too many people in leadership positions are afraid to step outside the box, fearing they will be embarrassed or appear to not look "corporate." As corporate processes have become more complex, some managers became afraid of what they don't know or that their employees might know more than they do. The reporting relationship became inverted, with managers substituting being a "nice guy/gal" to keep their people around, rather than inspiring them with positive leadership. Another reason is that the managers often refuse to learn enough of what is going on in their jobs, trying to finesse their way through (thus the increase in politicking) rather than embracing the general flow of processes for which they are responsible. As an example, a CEO of a Fortune 200 company is well regarded among employees as unassuming, a "great guy," "really nice," etc. But the performance of that company has been miserable, continually losing market share year after year with many missed opportunities, false starts, and poor customer service rankings that are among the worst in that industry. The simple reason? This CEO has found a comfort niche in being a "nice guy" and there is little accountability at this company for performance. He has left underperforming upper management in place so that he doesn't have to get involved in the areas mentioned above and this has further encouraged that same upper management to govern in the style as the CEO does.

There are cures to this. Certainly, there are ways to balance demand for performance with effective people skills. This book examines some things that successful leaders do...and also what unsuccessful ones do. I admit it up front: there is no scientific or journalistic research involved in this writing, just a listing of observations and their consequences that I have seen both as a junior officer in the US Army and as a salesman and sales leader in the corporate world.

Perhaps you find that you already do many of the things mentioned herein. Maybe you are now cognizant that you already practice some good leadership techniques. In that case, this book might reinforce those behaviors and give you some new ideas of how to further apply them.

On the other hand, if some of these tactics seem very strange and unholy to you, it might spur you on to think very deeply about just how much more successful you could be if you gave some of these ideas a try. It's never too late to become a better leader, even if only marginally. But also understand that a lot of small moves can add up to being a more effective leader in a big way.

One note for reading this book: I'm no sexist. While, for the sake of convenience, I usually use "him" and "his" as pronouns, I fully embrace gender equality in the workplace. The best (and worst) leaders I have known have been of both sexes.

CHAPTER 1

The Need for Leadership

Among all animals on the earth, including humans, the necessity and the effects of leadership are obvious. Every pride of lions, every gaggle of geese, every pack of wolves has its leaders, protecting the group and finding food and shelter. Sometimes, leadership roles in these animal groups rotate among various members, but there are always dominant individuals that spearhead the operations of the group.

Are humans different? Not at all. Just like the non-dominant animals belonging to the groups mentioned above, people need leadership. And they will accept and respect good leadership. Unlike in some animal groups, human leaders tend to stay dominant for most of their lives, rather than lead for a while then revert to being a non-leader. In other words, the playground leader often becomes senior class president and then leads in adult roles. We certainly all know exceptions to this role, where some schoolyard leaders never go much farther, and many people have no aspirations to any leadership position ever in their lives.

So do people crave good leadership? Yes, they do! Considering that politicians can be leaders, why are some US presidents held in such high esteem and others are not? There are always some neighbors who are more active in community affairs than others and seem to spearhead local initiatives and do it in a pleasant manner. Of course, there are some arrogant types who never accept any leadership at all. Some of these do well in life because of unusual skills, but we all know the anti-social, lone-wolf types who are pretty miserable to be around and who always try to thumb their noses at authority. These folks generally don't seem to end up very happy in their lives.

Most people will happily accept good leadership because they know it will improve their own lives. Good leadership will help them to be more successful in their jobs, becoming more productive and earning more money. This is perhaps most evident in the sales career fields, where good managers can give effective direction, leading to rapidly increasing sales, and often, higher incentive pay. Although the results may not be noticed as soon, good leadership can pay off for employees in all career fields as they increase their skills, their confidence, and their marketability. People know when they are well led. Outside the workplace, people accept good leadership because it makes for a more efficient, orderly, and prosperous society.

One of the strongest reasons to develop good leaders in any organization is that good leaders make good companies even better. It is easy to see that the opposite of this is true, that poor leadership can hurt a company badly. Recent examples of Enron, HealthSouth, and many others bear this point out strongly. Look at what strong corporate leadership has done for some companies, such as Jack Welch at General Electric, Herb Kelleher at Southwest Airlines, and the late

Roberto Goizueta at Coca-Cola. Although, at the highest levels, some of the practices in this book may not be practical to follow, they follow the principles used by these and other effective corporate leaders. And that can be summed up in one small statement: *Get the most you can from all your people and have them feel good about giving their best.*

While it is easy to point to good or bad corporate-level leadership, as it is often in the headlines and can affect stock prices, and is usually the most visible and interesting part of any company, this book will mainly concentrate on lower-level leadership. The skills needed by first – and second-level managers are not often codified or taught; many times, first-time leaders are thrown into a "sink-or-swim" situation. While many do well, the lessons learned are often painful and create inefficiencies. It is okay to stub your toe to learn a lesson, but breaking your leg is too painful, time-consuming, and expensive. And if that leg is broken in front of customers or team members, it can be even more costly.

Many of the techniques covered in this book become life-long habits of good leaders. They understand the value of basic, good leadership and use them in various ways as they climb the corporate ladder. These are really *people skills*, and they can be applied in many life situations, personal as well as business. In sales, it is a well-accepted truism that, other things being equal, **people buy from people they know and like.** That same principle applies to management opportunities in the corporate arena. Among those people who excel, the better opportunities will generally come to those with superior people skills.

So, on a macro level, why the real need for better corporate leadership in America? Just look at all the challenges facing us. Foreign competition, driven by lower labor costs, is sending jobs to former third-world environments. When you consider that lower labor costs are really a function of productivity (output per unit of labor), you can see why inspiring workers to higher levels of output can be so critical.

Another related challenge is the generally weaker dollar in the exchange markets. Most experts say that the era of the dominant dollar is gone forever and that the United States needs to get used to being a competitor in the global marketplace rather than the market maker we were for the last half of the twentieth century. And one of the keys to being a stronger competitor is to have better, more productive leaders running your business.

A more recent but very serious concern for American corporations is the rapid escalation of energy costs. Although it gets little play in the broad issue of energy, conservation in the workplace is a major opportunity for most companies to lower their energy bills, thus becoming more competitive overall. The spirit, ingenuity, and discipline of well-led employees can be a major factor in this effort.

And, finally, a large challenge to corporate America is the values and talents of most of our younger employees, known as Generations X and Y. Most of them came into their jobs with little sense of corporate loyalty and with a strong sense of entitlement. They feel justified in not acknowledging any corporate loyalty because the general sense is that the company treats them as a commodity and has no loyalty towards them. Often, they feel a sense of detachment, the feeling of their employment as simply a job instead of *what they do*. The feeling of entitlement comes from the fact that many of them have had few struggles in their lives; most grew up in middle-class America and have not experienced a great deal of hardship. On the other hand, these younger folks bring to the marketplace the best-educated, most computer-literate, most capable generation ever. The need for corporations to tap and retain this talent is of critical proportions. The future of American competitiveness hinges on it—the leadership techniques required to direct these folks is of huge importance.

There are obvious and significant benefits of good leadership:

- improved profits caused by more productive employees and reduced personnel turnover
- better morale, leading to inspired team performances
- mentorship will become an obvious opportunity as employees strive to be like their leaders.

But the most important benefit from good leadership comes by putting employees and their managers on the same side of the table, by narrowing the gulf between "labor" and "management." Inspired leadership will directly result in a great deal of respect being earned by managers and, even though employees may not personally like their manager, there will be a detectable air of respect in that relationship, and this will enhance the feelings of team identity.

Improving the leadership at first – and second-line levels is one of the greatest needs and opportunities for corporate America. It can be done in a low-cost, low-impact manner by simply adjusting the way we think about it. Read on...take the following challenges and try some of these ideas.

CHAPTER 2

The Definition of Leadership

Defining a concept is not easy. Personal qualities that do not lend themselves to direct and exact measurements are often overlooked to some extent as something that "you either have or you don't." As former Supreme Court justice Potter Stewart is reported to have said in trying to define pornography, "I can't define it, but I know it when I see it." Certainly, we all know good leadership when we see it. But even with all these subjective concerns, I think we can apply some standards on which we can all agree.

Probably the best definition I have ever heard is one of the earliest ones I ever experienced. As a young Army officer, I was required to memorize a definition similar to this one from a training manual. I have adapted it only slightly in the intervening years. This old definition has likely been updated over the years, but it still has application today.

Leadership is the art of influencing subordinate team members to elicit their willing and enthusiastic contribution toward achieving unit goals.

Seems very simple. Let's look at each part in more detail.

"the art": As mentioned in the opening of this chapter, this is not a science with clearly defined terms and limits. There is no one way to be an effective leader with easily measureable metrics. Leadership requires and encourages each person's individual techniques and flourishes. All potential managers will utilize their own personality strengths and their flaws will be demonstrated in defining their own brand of leadership. Often, manager candidates will try to model themselves after some famous leader; while in general terms this is okay, trying to be too much like somebody else rarely works well. I remember after the movie *Patton* was released, there was talk about corporate leaders trying to emulate the title role. Well, sometimes that approach doesn't even work in the Army. The time and the situation must be accommodating to a particular approach and the leaders cannot try to be someone they are not. While using some traits from a famous leader may work, don't even try to be too much like that leader because then you can't be you.

"influencing": A leader must use persuasive influence to get the job done right. Even when position power coerces employees to do what the boss demands, to get excellent results, you must *influence* your people. This lesson was brought home hard to me early on. As a young second lieutenant, I had a gold bar on my collar that signified a position of power—I was the platoon leader and had the force of law on my side. I could order a soldier to drop down and give me twenty pushups (not that I ever did). But the military is really not much different than the business world when it comes to leadership, except

certainly the stakes are higher. In business, poor leadership might mean loss of money; in war, poor leadership might mean loss of life.

The better way to use influence is to let the subordinates think that the initiative is their idea. It is not a command or an absolute order; the leader expresses a desired outcome, gives the subordinate as little direction as needed, supplies the resources, then lets the employee do the work with as little direct supervision as needed. Again, using the military example, I soon realized that many of the sergeants in my platoon had been in the Army longer than I had been on earth. Some had been in combat in Vietnam. How would they feel about taking direct orders from a twenty-two–year-old kid? That is where a lot of the second lieutenant jokes come from. (The difference between a second lieutenant and a private E2? The E2 has been promoted once! I heard that one a few times.) A lot more things got done with higher-quality results when the sergeants were allowed to run the platoon, with the young officer's job being to establish goals and provide resources and a certain degree of oversight. Some of the sergeants required a little more direct supervision than others; probably the most difficult part for me was to decide how much was needed. But when they felt empowered, when I complemented their authority rather than subverting it, they accomplished their tasks more quickly and with higher quality.

Another challenge in this area is to lead from the front, but not in such a way as to grab the spotlight from the subordinate leaders and those doing the work. A sales manager must go on sales calls, an operations manager must have at least a basic understanding of what processes his people use, a maintenance manager should spend some time in the service areas. Someone who seldom shows up at the place where his people work will never muster much respect from the team. In other words, be a part of your team; don't try to rule from the top. A manager who leads from the front inspires confidence in the entire corporate system and promotes strong feelings of team membership.

"subordinate team members": Despite this phrase in the definition, any employee under your direct or indirect reporting relationship should be considered a full *team member*, and should never be referred to as a subordinate or an underling, or any other word that has a negative connotation. After all, we need these folks to get the job done; we can't do it without them. Giving them this small dignity will work wonders, and it can accomplished with just a little thoughtful effort.

You should try to make your people feel like they are owners—certainly, they are part owners of the company, whether or not they own stock. They are owners because they have a direct impact on and a significant interest in how well the company does. But, more importantly, *they own what they do.* This distinction means that the manager trusts them to do it right, to make their contribution, however small, in the most efficient and effective way. If you can get the point across that the team member owns his process, you will create the atmosphere that allows your employees to take pride in a job well done. They will truly feel like owners, not peons.

Be sure to always play up the word *"team."* Just as people can behave badly in a crowd, such as suggested by mob mentality, they perform in a spectacular fashion when they feel they are part of a winning team that is well-led. Notice how within hours, sports fans will wear the newest caps and T-shirts celebrating a recent championship—people identify with winning teams. How might their job performance improve if they felt they worked for a winning company?

"elicit their willing contributions": The goal of this part is to have your employees deliver because they *want to*, not because they *have to.* As mentioned above, you can give orders to get tasks done. But a team member who gives a willing contribution is much more likely to do the job in a high-quality fashion and in a more cheerful way that improves overall team morale as well. Often, they will give effort above minimum requirements.

One of the ways to accomplish this is to recognize and appreciate all good efforts, even those that fail. A good example of this comes from baseball, where even the best hitters will fail about 70 percent of the time. The goal of a good hitter is not necessarily to swing for the fences, but to hit sharp, solid line drives. Fly balls will usually be caught for outs and grounders may not make it through the infield. But hard line drives are the most likely routes to hits, and the best hitters know how to turn a large percentage of their swings into them. Let's assume that every batter is trained, incented, and has the right attitude to a hit line drive every time he swings. Even still, a hard line drive might go straight to the shortstop and be caught for an out. This is not a bad turn at the plate; the batter did all he could do. But if the player continues to hit line drives, the hits will come and he will be a superb batter. This analogy holds in every business situation. Those team members that have the right training, incentives, and attitude will hit line drives every time; they will do all the right things to make their contributions successful. The effort should always be applauded, even if the end result was not a true success. This will further incent similar future efforts and encourage the employee to go above and beyond the job description.

So how do you applaud non-successes? Again, the key is to recognize the effort, conduct an after-action review of what went right, and give credit to the team members who did all the right things. Focus in on what the team member could have done to further improve the odds of success. After all, this is what you want to have happen consistently in your organization.

When they give their best effort, people tend to feel good about themselves and the company. Those who slack and cut corners will be found to have poor morale and probably poor self-esteem. Good effort will become an addiction that will improve all factors in the workplace.

But successes must come or your company will go out of business. If your team hits lots of line drives but does not experience much success, you, as a leader, must re-evaluate the process to see why more success cannot be obtained from superior efforts.

"achieving unit goals": No revelation here: all unit goals should be known, measurable, reachable, and flexible. Goals should be known at least to all those in the unit that shares those goals; you might consider some sharing of that information to inspire good-natured rivalries among various groups. For example, a sales team with a dollar target for margin might be in a "race" with an operations unit that is striving to reduce the number of billing errors. The prize might be a pizza lunch, a half day off, or something like that. Measurable goals seem intuitive, but some have a problem with the concepts of reachable and flexible. A reachable goal should not be slam-dunk easy, yet it should not be thought of as impossible, either. The concern is that annual goals set in January might seem ridiculously high to some team members at that early stage of the year; if they had the foresight to consider where they might be in October, the goal might seem more achievable. To keep your team from losing spirit in this situation, try to break the goals down into shorter time frames (maybe quarterly?) whenever possible. Or perhaps a large production goal can be broken into increments. This also ties in to the spirit of flexibility. You might consider lowering goals when forces outside the control of your team influence events. For example, in the power business, one year we had to put severe restrictions on the sales team for quantity to be sold and we had to allocate sales by highest margin. If we had stuck to our original plan for variable compensation, we would have lost many valuable and experienced sales professionals. But we adjusted goals and incented the team to sell what they could at the higher margins. When the situation returned to normal, the sales force was appreciative of this gesture; it seemed to deepen their dedication to the team and lowered our anticipated employee attrition to competitors. On the other hand, should you

ever increase goals when outside forces make goal attainment easier? It can be done, but approach it carefully and all the implications should be carefully thought out. For example, again from the power business, a competitor had laid out a variable compensation plan for their sales force that seemed reasonable. The plan would pay about eighty thousand dollars or so annually in incentive if the salesperson reached a total margin of two million dollars. But the planners failed to realize that two million dollars in that new market was a piece of cake; some salespeople accomplished over five million dollars in margin. So, at the end of the plan year, the company reneged on the plan and capped payments at a certain level. The reason given to the sales force was, "We can't pay you more than our executives." You can imagine how that went over. That company's business in that market segment was damaged for many years into the future. Perhaps some sort of compromise as early as possible, when it seemed like the team would blow away its goals, would have worked better. For example, third- and fourth-quarter goals could have been increased while paying the agreed-upon compensation for the earlier parts of the year.

This definition of leadership, while probably not perfect, should give you a better understanding of one unmistakable fact: good leadership does not just happen. Although it may be easier for some than others, it requires a lot of planning and painstaking execution. Are some people good joke-tellers? Yes, but consider that most individuals write down their jokes on index cards and practice them. *Every human endeavor that is worth something requires effort and planning.*

CHAPTER 3

CHARACTERISTICS OF GOOD LEADERS

The good leader is constantly and consistently selling himself to the team, just as one would to an external customer—not in an overt and superficial sort of manner, but in a way that shows the subordinates that the leader is always there, is trustworthy, cares about them and their welfare, and wants to do the right thing for the long-term growth of both the company and the employees. In selling yourself as a leader, you don't want to seem forced on the team; you want the team to "buy" you as opposed to "renting" you. What's the difference? When someone makes a commitment to buy something, they embrace it, identify with it, and try their best to make it work. But if you rent something, there is the clear implication that the relationship is temporary, that you can more easily replace it, and commitment is not needed. Another leader will come along later. It seems obvious that the team is more productive and interrelationships are more positive when the leader is "bought" by the group.

There are some things the leader can do to be "bought." One important quality is **self-assurance**. A good leader knows that he is valued by the company and that if the team performs, his future is secure. Recognition and rewards will be given to the leader if the team is successfully led and meeting or exceeding all its goals. Any company that doesn't recognize that basic fact is setting itself up for turbulence and instability in the ranks, as perceptions and politics become more important than rewarding good leadership. Backstabbing and gossip will replace loyalty and true effort that is dedicated to goal achievement. As president, Ronald Reagan had a desk plaque that said, "There is no limit to the amount of good a man can do if he doesn't stop to worry about who gets the credit." Would you want to work for a company that manages its leaders any other way?

Something to understand is the difference between self-assurance and cockiness. Being self-assured means being a little quieter, letting your actions do the talking, letting the team have the spotlight for its successes. The leader should still lead from the front but is clearly the power behind the team. A cocky leader will often hog the limelight, will take team accomplishments and try to convince upper management that he did it all himself. Haven't we all seen this poor example of leadership? There is no quicker way to deflate team spirit than this.

Another important quality in the good leader is **optimism**. The leader must be able to pick up the team, even when he is down. And this optimism must be truly felt, even if a bit hokey. A good example of this happened to me at Army basic training. In the middle of a long, four-day field exercise, we were all pretty much tired, sweaty, hungry, and miserable. Just when you think it couldn't get any worse, it started to rain...and rain hard. So right when we were all about to give up and join the Commies (I was in the Army a long time ago), our team leader, a captain about forty years old at the time, walked around with his arms outstretched and said, "Guys, isn't this great? A free shower!" And then gave his standard line, "This Army is alllll-right." Now, how hokey can you get? This guy had been out in the field as long as the rest of us under the same conditions, but he earned the right to be respected as our leader from that moment. His optimism was meant to inspire us, to show us that bad things are simply problems to be worked out. There are many ways the business leader can show optimism, but they all start in the same place—by making sure the team knows that they can solve this problem and the leader will be there to help them. Your optimistic spirit leaves the team with a strong sense that, even though there are problems, we *can* get this job done.

It is critical that efficient leaders understand and exhibit **planning.** You've all heard the "5 Ps": "Proper Planning Prevents Poor Performance." (In the military, they often speak of the "6 Ps," with an extra modifier for the word "poor," but let's keep this clean and ignore that.) Planning can be boiled down into two components: short term and long term. In the short term, the leader is concerned about production goals, personnel issues, daily training, motivation of his team, and other items that are required to keep the business flowing. But the key is that he is *always planning for the short term.* The good leader always has contingency plans, such as what he does when certain things go wrong (as they will). He is continuously planning for ways to overcome obstacles, both expected and unexpected. Having contingency plans in place, and being ready to go when the obstacle appears, is a great way to show the team that you are very effective as their leader. For example, the team is well into a project and a key team member gets a better offer from your competitor and quits abruptly. Good short-term planning means that you have already thought about the loss of any key team member and you have a temporary solution ready to roll out that includes keeping the team on track for goal accomplishment and limiting the damage that this former employee can do with the competitor. When the team sees how smoothly the leader has negotiated this obstacle and, more importantly, how their goals can seemingly still be met despite the obstacle, their respect for the leader will grow.

As for long-term planning, this concerns things like keeping a "farm team" of potential recruits, training team members on longer-term strategic issues, integration of this team with other functions into the company structure, efficiency improvements, etc. The key difference between long- and short-term planning is that short-term planning should be done continuously, but long-term planning can be done in batches. While long-term planning can be put off for a quiet time, it cannot be ignored. A good leader should devote at least an hour a week to long-term planning issues.

In addition, good leaders show **proficiency** in the work process. Notice I say "proficiency" and not necessarily "expertise." The team members must know their jobs well, to the point of being experts in their own particular area, and the leader is responsible for getting them the training necessary to be that way. But the leader is responsible, sometimes on his own, for being knowledgeable over this whole process that he supervises, what each person's job is, and how it fits into the big picture. You simply can't get that way without immersing yourself in many, but not necessarily all, of the details. There are certain basic facts in every business that you must learn to be respected by your team members. For example, I had a boss in the electric business that never bothered to get comfortable with understanding the difference between a kilowatt and a kilowatt-hour. While this may puzzle some of you who are unfamiliar with electricity, it is a very basic concept of that business. As you can imagine, he didn't perform at a very high level and was not respected much. The good leader has total command of the information flow throughout his group and knows how his group fits into the larger organization.

Don't be afraid to get your hands dirty. Learn some details; team members love it when you ask them how they do their jobs.

Another important trait is the **willingness to get involved.** The leader who sits behind the desk all day and displays no outward interest in the team and its efforts will not earn their respect. Give an effort to get to know as many team members as possible by name, and if the team is not too large, try to learn family members' names and other personal items. Ask them about their vacation, how their kid is doing in school, how they like their new cubicle location, or if they have any pets. Interest in and involvement with people are vital, but the most important part of this quality is to get involved in job-performance issues. First, always be there to help with situations when the team member doesn't know how to proceed or when an unusual situation occurs and the employee doesn't know what to do or feels they need approval to act. Even if you don't know what to do yourself, or even if the problem has no good answer, make sure the employee knows that you're in this with him and will do what you can to help. A poor example of leadership in this area regularly occurred when a former boss of mine was so concerned about getting home every day that he would walk down the hallway at five o'clock, passing many employees who had pending emails into him or requests to see him for help on business issues. The team members were willing to stay at least a little bit late to move the business forward, but the boss couldn't be bothered. I will never forget the look on their faces as he walked briskly past them, face lowered, the clear implication being that he didn't care about their issues. Just a few extra minutes would have meant so much to them.

But the leader cannot get too close to the team, either. There needs to be just enough separation so as to not accept lame excuses or to be able to efficiently impose disciplinary action when necessary. Always lead with the carrot, but recognize that the stick may be needed. And never assume that the team will perform to your expectations without your checking up on them as often as needed. Many team members may resent your "looking over their shoulder" even if done occasionally, but a good way to get their acquiescence and support for your oversight function is to provide feedback on what you observe... especially positive feedback on jobs done well.

Another invaluable asset is a **good sense of humor.** I'm not talking about a stand-up comedian, but an unassuming yet strong desire to make the workplace fun and fresh every day. The self-assured, confident leader often uses some mild self-deprecation as a source of humor (for example, when puzzling over a problem, "Gee, I'm not sure...this is the first time I've had a job for more than a day"). The key to poking fun at yourself (or anyone else) is that if the statement is so outrageous that it cannot possibly be true, it will become obvious to the team that it is intended to be humorous and no bad feelings will result. In other words, the jab is so far-fetched, it does not have an edge and is perceived by all as innocuous. In addition, be sure that the intended target of the jab will also be amused by the comment. Truly, some people are so sensitive that you can never use them in your story, no matter how unbelievable it may be. A problem can result if the comment strikes too close to the truth or to rumors of the truth. For example, if one individual who has a reputation of being flirtatious comes in late from lunch and a comment is made such as, "Oh, I thought you were out on a date," the intended humor in this remark might easily strike the wrong chord as many might think it is intended to verify the rumors. So, if you intend personal jabs, be sure they are obvious jokes at those who can take a little good-natured ribbing. And always use yourself as a target just as often as anyone else.

So how do you come across (and remember) funny material? The remembering is the easy part: when you come across something that you think might amuse the team, write it down or clip it out. I have always kept a file in my desk for humorous stories that I can browse through quickly. A good source of material is the comics from your newspaper. Many of the jokes can be re-used in almost any situation in the workplace. Also, just look up "jokes" on the Internet. Many of them are clearly out of bounds, but many will suffice. While using a couple of quick bits of humor during the day can lighten things up, try to lead off team meetings with a "story." Upper management is always a target appreciated by employees, and, again, I would hope your management would be self-assured enough to allow a little harmless fun at their expense. Here is a good story to use:

The vice president was talking to the CEO recently and the VP commented about the CEO's fancy shoes. The CEO said, "These are alligator shoes...all the important people in this company wear alligator shoes." Shortly after that, the VP and I were on a business trip to New Orleans and we were driving by some swampy areas. He says, "Stop the car right here." I was puzzled, but always do as I'm told, so I pulled over. The VP gets out of the car and says, "Wait here. I'll be back in a few minutes." So about fifteen minutes later, he comes back to the car, he's all muddy, his clothes are ripped, and he is bruised and bloodied. I'm shocked and I ask him, "What happened?" He replied, "Just my luck. I came across this big alligator, almost killed me to get him flipped over, then I see that he was barefoot."

A little humor among the team will keep them sharp and create a fun workplace that helps in retaining your best talent.

An effective leader will also **emphasize pride** in everyday work and your environs. Even the smallest things that he and the team do should be considered important. When walking in the work area, do you ever stop to pick up a piece of trash on the floor? Do you replace the water cooler bottle when it gets empty (assuming you are strong enough for that)? People see those things and respect your emphasis on a clean and enjoyable workspace for all. It also shows that you're not too good to do a menial task that benefits the team.

I was responsible for our lease and the office for about twenty-five people. The landlord did a pretty poor job; the office temperatures often varied widely from area to area and the restrooms were poorly ventilated. The attitude I saw upon arriving at this job was one of ambivalence, that they couldn't do much to fix the problems. This resulted in a drop in pride and morale, and, of course, this negatively affected team performance. I pushed the landlord hard to improve the situation and much improvement was made. The team saw me lying flat on the floor checking to see how much air was moving under the restroom door. By keeping the team informed of what I was doing, and by soliciting their input and asking if the improvements were helping, this now became a point of pride in our workplace. We were in this effort together and we would win together. These small victories tend to be infectious; they lead to a spirit of accomplishment. Pride, both individual and group, is one of the greatest motivators for your team members, as strong as compensation in many cases. It is a self-reinforcing cycle of success: anticipating, working towards, experiencing, and recognizing success.

You should allow team members to feel the pride of accomplishment, of being part of a winning team that is doing something important. You may have heard the story about the bricklayers. A guy walks up to the first one and asks what he is doing. The man replies rather glumly, "I'm laying bricks." When asking the second one the same question, the man stops for a second, looks off into the distance and says, "I'm building a great cathedral." Always try to inspire your team members to be that second bricklayer!

One more attribute of good leaders is **humility**. Yes, you may be the leader, but you're still human and if you are self-assured and good at your job, you don't mind letting the team know that you're a team member also; you just have a different position on the team. So steer clear of two potential traps in this area. First, don't make your employees seem anything less than you. So you have an office and they have cubicles? That may be necessary, but don't overemphasize it. Just refer to everyone's workplace (including yours) as a "desk" and don't use words like "office" or "cubicle." Don't refer to people as "yours," such as in the way my boss once introduced me: "He is *my* director of sales." Your people don't belong to you. Second, when introducing yourself when team members are present (and maybe even when they are not), just say that you're a team member (for example, "I'm Joe Smith and I'm in the billing group"). The team knows your position, but they appreciate that you identify yourself as one of them, not as their master. Have lunch or take breaks with your employees as often as you can; establish commonality, again being careful not to get so close as to blur your objectivity. Tell them as much as you can about corporate and market happenings, giving as much information as you can without divulging secrets. You'd be surprised how few employees understand the reasons for certain corporate announcements. By taking some time to explain *why* things are done, the team will come to appreciate your position and your knowledge of the business. This will strengthen their respect for you as a leader. Respect is to be valued over likeability, and you cannot worry too much about being liked. But most respected leaders are well thought of by their team members. (Read up on Omar Bradley, the "soldier's general.") On the other hand, not many of Patton's soldiers liked him...but they liked being on his successful team, as they got more than their share of the headlines. President Obama refers to his grandfather's service in WWII with the statement, "He was in Patton's Army." Many of these veterans feel that way, not because they liked Patton, but because they were a part of one of the most successful forces in the history of mankind.

You can indirectly share some of the burdens of leadership. For example, when you must discharge an employee, you can let people know how difficult that is without giving details of the situation that caused the dismissal. Not many people understand the rigors of managing people and thus they can respect your feelings in this area.

Regarding self-assuredness, nobody likes working for the stuffed-shirt, corporate politician—the guy who is so worried about looking good and not making any mistakes that he stifles creativity and bores his team. American business experts agree that one of the best corporate leaders ever was Herb Kelleher, the former CEO at Southwest Airlines. Kelleher was famous for doing "outrageous" things, like dressing up in a bunny outfit (think "rabbit," not "Playboy") and walking around and talking to workers on the tarmac. If you do regard this episode as "outrageous," you may have some humility issues to work on; people respond to leadership like this.

A good leader truly **cares about his people.** You can't fake this. Your subordinates are people just like you, with their own lives, and they should all be respected. Poor leaders look upon themselves as a bit superior to their people (see the part on humility, above) or perhaps they think that the purpose of subordinates is to support their leader's career ambitions. I assure you, the team members don't feel that way.

Let's assume that, as a leader, you really do care about your team. So how do you show it? One easy way is to say exactly that. In private meetings, there will be ample opportunities, many times a year, to simply look at them and say, "I care about you." You can add another sentence or two, such as, "And I want to help you to get better" in the case of someone who is struggling, or maybe, "And I'm glad you're on our team." Those words, if meant earnestly, will pay big dividends for retention and boosting the loyalty of your team. Also, with just a little bit more effort, you can demonstrate your care in other strong ways. Ask your HR department for a roster of your team with their service anniversaries and birthdays on it. How about sending just a brief email (two sentences) on those two special days for them? You could copy other group members in a manner of publicizing the remembrance, but I have had greater results with just a private email, probably because it doesn't appear to other team members to be a public exclamation of "look what a nice boss I am" and that you're sucking up to the team. But either way, it is something they will really appreciate. If you want to go a step further, a handwritten note from you, for these events or any other small accomplishments, is always a winner. If you have a departmental newsletter, how about incorporating some of these acknowledgments in there? But beware of false or belittling praise. The old joke in the Army about a poor performance review holds that your commanding officer says, "You usually dress well and are seldom late." Make sure the deed is of reasonable value and that, if publicized, it will be appreciated by all who see it. Being recognized in almost any positive way makes people feel valued and makes them feel that the boss cares about them.

A very important quality is that a good leader is **trusted** by his team members. Integrity cannot be compromised and you must avoid any and all situations that might lead to even the slightest perception of mistrust. Most executive offices nowadays do not provide total privacy...we all know why there are windows. But that is part of the transparency that all good leaders endorse. No hidden agendas, what you see is what you get, plain speaking, etc.—just like in a John Wayne movie, these are some of the qualities upon which respect and trust are built. Keeping a secret is critical; you must totally resist the urge to think you can improve your popularity at the expense of divulging private information, just as you must resist those who want you to share the scoop. One way to do this is, after being asked for gossip fodder, is to take the person aside and ask, "Can you keep a secret?" Of course they will answer in the affirmative (as if they would ever say they could not keep a secret). Then you simply tell them, "So can I." That person will probably not ask you for private information again. Or you can say something like, "You know I can't talk about that." Do you have a rumor-mill issue at your company? If so, address it head on with a comment like, "If you didn't hear it from me, it probably didn't happen." And tales of your trustworthiness and sense of honor will spread, not only within your team, but among your superiors as well.

An attribute of good leaders is a sense of **energy**. This enthusiasm is contagious among anyone who comes in contact with you. Even on bad days, focus on the positive and think of ways to make yourself peppier and livelier. We all know people who seem to suck the energy out of the room. They pooh-pooh any and all new ideas and they have an attitude that the world is against all of us...enough already. Stop that talk. Take them aside if needed, but make sure that everyone knows that we can each make a difference. Even if only in a small way each day, if we all do just a little more, by keeping an energetic spirit just think of the cumulative improvements we can make. Would you rather be around the Energizer Bunny or Eeyore the donkey?

Another important characteristic is the ability to **eliminate** "groupthink" and total paralysis by needing consensus on most every decision. I was in a company like this...nothing got done and the business suffered for it. And the cause was simple: the leaders were afraid to try anything new, had no real confidence in their own abilities, and wanted to ensure that any blame from the consequences of a bad decision would not rest solely on their shoulders. These "leaders" would de-emphasize accountability by spreading out the decision over many departments that might have only peripheral responsibility for that area. This situation is further described later in this book.

The ways to eliminate groupthink are fairly straightforward. First, and most importantly, every good leader *knows the business and has an intuition as to the direction the business needs to follow for growth.* This seems simple, but is far too often disregarded in the appointment of leaders. For example, in the deregulated electric power business, some of these companies were formed from the old electric utilities. There is a huge difference in the two business models. In the monopoly utility model, there are no customers, only ratepayers who have no choice of provider. But in the deregulated scenario, customers have a choice and they can choose to leave you for another provider. In many cases, the former utilities moved many of their leaders to the deregulated world, often due to the "old-boy" and patron-based networks. Many of these people could not put the conceptual difference between "ratepayer" and "customer" into their mindset, and this often resulted in poor performance by some companies who should have done much better in the competitive marketplace. Think of some of the dichotomies. In the utilities, decisions could take longer, as there was no competitor trying to take away your business. Also, the virtual "employment-for-life" perception often seen in utilities caused many of them to work with the same people for many years, resulting in an inability and unwillingness to force decisions on their long-time friends. So, the better-performing companies after deregulation had many leaders who had the competitive mindset required to run a customer-centric company. It is easy to claim that you are centered around your customers, but harder to make it happen. It requires all levels of leadership to put customers first every day, ahead of most other things. And by "intuition," I don't mean using palm readers and a Ouija board. Start by asking yourself one question that should become a mantra for any successful business: *"If I were the customer, would I buy this?"* Think about the short- and long-term implications of the decision: will they lead to acquiring more customers AND retaining more customers AND making your customers more profitable? You must have all three.

Another method for eliminating groupthink is to build consensus, but not in large or inter-department meetings. Meet with key stakeholders, especially among your subordinates, individually or in small groups. In this fashion, they will feel freer to voice their concerns and opinions than in a larger group, and the leader can address those concerns more thoroughly. In smaller group settings, the leader can use his personal power of persuasion more effectively, without the obvious display of position power that a large, formal meeting suggests.

When it comes time to announce the decision, that decision should be made to the entire team that is affected. If the leader has done his preparation work as described above, then most stakeholders already feel part of the process and the solution, and they will embrace the plan, hopefully, as if it were their own idea. In any case, state your belief that the implementation and resulting success is a big team effort and the contributions of all are required to reach the destination.

And, finally, an absolutely critical attribute of good leadership, perhaps the most important of all, is to be a good **communicator.** Of course, everyone thinks they are a good communicator, just like everyone thinks they are a good driver. But, as we all know, there are lots of bad drivers out there on the roads and really good communicators are not very common. A few points to facilitate effective communications:

- Put yourself in the shoes of the recipient of the message. Would you understand your message if you were that person? Would it motivate you? Consider the recipient's position, experience, education, etc. when constructing your message, whether written or oral. A manager on my team was truly one of the smartest people I'd ever met…but for him, this was both a blessing and a curse. He had difficulty in adjusting his message to be understood by those who didn't have the same grasp of the situation as he had. It was a continuous battle for him to be empathic enough so that all could embrace, understand, and be motivated by his message.

- Listen, listen, and listen. Don't just hear and read people's words; *discern their message.*

- In the case of written communications, never send one without a final proofreading, and, if possible, write the message the day before you send it so you can sleep on it. This seems elementary, but we all know that poorly constructed emails are death to good leadership because they are often sent with little review.

- For oral communications, rehearse *every* proposed conversation to the greatest extent possible. When you see a team member approaching, even a simple "good morning" can be more effective by mentioning a spouse's or child's name, or by bringing up a recent event. When you can, jot down a few notes about the oral message you want to convey so that all points can be covered efficiently without requiring revisits or creating misunderstandings.

- As mentioned elsewhere in this book, you must be courageous and get out of your comfort zone. Are there people you'd just rather avoid? We all have them, but if you don't approach and communicate with them in just the same way as others, it can cause others to see your bias. It is likely that team members feel the same way about the difficult employee, but your magnanimity and courage will be another reason the team respects your leadership.

This seems to be a pretty full list. But if the desire to be a good leader is there and you have at least some amount of willingness to try new things, most people can accomplish and flourish by using them.

CHAPTER 4

Characteristics of Good Followers

The essential rule to remember about your team members, as well as all people, is *"they love to buy, but they hate to be sold."* For those in sales arenas, that sounds a lot like a customer, doesn't it? The parallels are significant—in a very large way, your subordinate is your customer; you are offering things for him to "buy," and the team's success depends on how willingly and thoroughly he "purchases" your directives, ideas, and goals. This is in no way meant to imply that the team members rule the roost and that the leader must kiss up to them to get them to work. Not at all. But it does recognize that the leader can play a big role in how well a job gets done.

For much of this chapter, think of yourself as both a follower and a leader. Because, after all, you have a boss and he expects you to function as his team member. How well you take higher-level directives and accomplish your missions with your resources and your team is an indication of your ability and willingness to be a good follower.

Here's another example. When a younger person is promoted to management of a team, there is the constant choice between when to use position power and when to use personal power. Most of the team are older and with much more job experience. So how does a young leader get effective control of a group like this? Yes, you have the *position power* to order them to do things; you probably can discipline or fire them. In fact, early in their management careers, many of your peers will rely almost exclusively on position power and their experienced workers will pretend to get the job done. There will be so many issues with poor performance because they will seldom go beyond the job description and there will likely be constant sniping and battling among the ranks. But the wiser young managers quickly learn that the workers (and thus the whole unit) perform much better if *you let them think it was their idea.* Instead of giving an order, it just takes a few seconds longer to talk to them quietly and make suggestions as to what needs to be done. Ask them how they might do it and what you can do to help. Make sure the resources for the job are present or tell them how they might obtain what is needed. As mentioned previously, the leader has to know the job and how to do it, but by relying on the experience of your subordinate managers and the key expertise of the individuals, you will find that they will embrace the mission and do a better job. The key is asking them, not telling them, and using your *personal power* more than your position power.

A good example from my military days: My platoon's squad leaders and I were looking at a map over the hood of a Jeep (yes, I'm old... way before the days of the Humvee). I was thinking about where each squad needed to move as we made our way towards the objective. I had made the decision early on that I wanted one of the squads to occupy some high ground on the eastern edge of our approach vector. I could have easily said something like, "Sergeant Jones, take your squad to an overwatch position on this hill," as I pointed to the place on the map. We had a few minutes, so instead I asked the squad leaders, "We need first squad in an overwatch position somewhere to the east...any ideas?" It was obvious that there were several good locations, but which one? Sergeant Jones suggested he take his squad to a certain area that he identified on the map; it was close to what I thought was perfect but not quite. I responded with something like, "That's a good idea, but this hill right next to it seems a little higher and would give a better view. What do you think?" He agreed and we proceeded with the exercise. What was the difference in the two ways to approach the directive to move his squad? In the second example, it was now Sergeant Jones' idea; he was part of the decision and he would run with it and embrace it much more fully than if he were simply told what to do.

Your people need to be mature and understand that sometimes an absolute order will come down with little leeway for performance. But by showing them that you want and value their input, you will give them a sense of empowerment that will lead to higher enthusiasm and better results on the task. That level of empowerment can be tailored to their experience level and can be monitored as required to ensure completeness and high quality. A good follower understands that opportunities like this are important and he is ready to make suggestions to help the team.

There is another parallel between employees and customers regarding the characteristics of followers: customers will always invite you back if they enjoy your visit and they learn something. This is important in leadership, also. Your team members want to learn and grow in their field. And they want to have fun on the job. If they go home every evening feeling like they have learned something, enjoyed the day, and profited from your leadership, your retention and performance issues will be much improved.

Followers must be willing to give up some of their individuality to be part of the team. Obviously, the military is one of the biggest examples of this, where uniforms are mandatory and many parts of life are strictly controlled. Even future officers must attend "boot camp," the purpose of which is to make them good followers and good team players before they can become good leaders. The US Army also expects its members to charge uphill to capture objectives while being shot at and the Catholic Church expects its clergy to be celibate. It is doubtful that you will ask for anything quite as drastic of your team members! I guess the best analogy is that of a baseball team. It takes all nine players working as a team to win the game. Some may want to be the pitcher, some the shortstop, but somebody's got to play right field. And, with batting, somebody will be called on the make the sacrifice bunt and not be allowed to swing away. You will not be able to let each team member play the marquee role all the time and some will get frustrated that they "never" get to be the star. That's where good communication skills are critical. The good leader will sense that some teammates are chafing by being team players and will talk to them privately to reassure them of their worth in their position and why that role is critical to team success.

Team members also give up some of their individuality when you ask them to share information. As we all know, open sharing of important information is the lifeblood of every organization, and employees should be acknowledged and rewarded when they share what they could have hoarded. Attendance at after-work events is another part of this area. Some teams really gel when they get a good attendance at these functions, whether they are team-building or charitable in nature. Whenever possible, schedule an event like this and encourage your team to participate. When subordinates truly accept your leadership (they have *bought* you), they are more willing to give more to the job, they don't look at the clock as much, and they accept and enjoy all work-related activities. A good example of this is scheduling your group to work a charity function or some other service project.

Another characteristic of good followers is that they are willing to accept leadership. Sounds like common sense, right? But we all know those individuals who are always sniping and second-guessing the boss. They haven't accepted leadership, and their motives may be personal ambition or they could just be general malcontents. Remember the words of Abraham Lincoln, who is reported to have said, "Most people are about as happy as they make their minds up to be." But, usually, the better the leader, the fewer of these malcontents are on the team. Only the most hardened cynics or backstabbers can refuse the positive aura that a first-class leader brings to the group. As other team members revel in the glow of good leadership, the malcontent usually sees he is the only one unhappy and that often tempers his poor outlook.

A good follower can be upwardly mobile and desiring of promotions for himself, yet still have the maturity to know that a good leader can make him better in his job and, ultimately, more valuable to the organization. That is because good followers understand that their career is a marathon, not a sprint, and that time spent honing their craft under good supervision is critical. Strong team members who are saddled with a poor leader will often think to themselves, "I could do better than that if I were in the job." But the mature follower will recognize when good leadership is broadening his horizons and making him better at his job.

Can a manager promoted from within the group succeed with his old peers now being his subordinates? Usually, the answer is "yes," assuming a few prerequisites. First, while serving on the team, was the former peer one of the higher performers? Within a team, everyone knows who pulls the wagon and who only rides. And the obvious politicians, those who spend more effort looking good than being good, are labeled quickly as well. Within most teams, there is an individual or two who display leadership among their peers. Without position power, they are a source of knowledge, morale, and teamwork that peers recognize, and that makes the team run more smoothly. These types of team members can usually be promoted and be expected to be successful as the new leader. One potential pitfall is to be expecting some jealousy from those not promoted. It is best for both the higher-level manager and the newly promoted leader to have private proactive meetings with any and all team members that might be suspected of harboring ill feelings about not getting the promotion. During these meetings, a candid and honest discussion about why the actions were taken should be held. Most people can handle the truth; it just needs to be explained clearly and privately to them. As long as they can be assured their career is progressing, they will usually accept the new leader or at least give him enough support to give him a chance at being successful.

Good followers can see the larger picture beyond their own immediate self-interest. They know that their contributions are appreciated and important because the leader *shows* this on a regular basis. Although compliments and rewards are not handed out unless deserved, the leader will often praise good work (remember, praise publicly and criticize privately). Subordinates all need to have a growth plan whereby they and the leader agree that certain attainment of goals, skills, and other criteria will result in career progression in some fashion. Some of the most difficult employees are those that do something well one time and immediately want a raise and promotion. There should be clear understanding during private conversations between leader and subordinate that all these areas must be clearly accomplished: job skill attainment, surpassing minimum and "stretch" goals, regularly demonstrating teamwork, learning the greater context of the business, how his job fits into the overall perspective, and how the company makes its money...and many other job performance objectives and criteria that can be added here. And it all must be consistent, with few instances of regression. Why not draw it out into a type of roadmap?

The key to this is that the leader sits down with the employee on a regular basis and assesses their long-term progress on these tasks. It is appropriate to give recognition and small rewards upon demonstration of this growth. It should be done in a fairly general way so that any private goals the employee has (particular to him, which other employees may not have) are de-emphasized. For example, if your subordinate has a remedial type of goal, such as to adopt a more pleasant attitude, come in to work on time, etc., don't tell everyone you are giving a certificate for that, but encompass all things that person has done right into a general laudatory comment. When employees see a plan and can measure their progress against the plan, they are inclined to be more productive and less anxious about job stagnation. However, leaders are strongly cautioned that any rewards they imply from meeting the objectives of a "roadmap" are not promised, but that meeting the objectives makes the team member eligible for further consideration. Be careful not to promise what you cannot deliver!

I think the biggest key to accepting leadership and being a good follower takes diplomatic skill on the part of both parties. Many times, the leader and a subordinate leader will have a legitimate disagreement on a path to be taken. Their positions and experiences will not allow them to see the problem in the same light. For example, let's say the choice of a new operating system is being made and one party wants brand X and other brand Y. At those times, the leader should have the patience and skill to take the subordinate leader aside privately and explain (to the greatest extent that time and propriety permit) his decision to go with brand X. Then, the skill of the good subordinate leader takes over; he must leave that meeting and embrace the idea of brand X *as if it were his own idea.* That is the hard part. The subordinate leader must not give grudging support to the idea, harboring his resentment and giving lukewarm endorsements of the plan to his subordinate team or peers. A great response to them might be, "It's a very good plan and we can do it." At a minimum, the subordinate leader might tell his team, "You know there were many ideas being considered. But this is a good plan, and we will all give a hundred percent to get it done right." *As if it were your own idea.*

As a leader, use the skills of your team. Consider how much good they can contribute towards the objectives rather than being concerned about what they cannot do.

CHAPTER 5

SELECTION CONSIDERATIONS FOR POTENTIAL LEADERS

In choosing someone to be a leader, your selection criteria obviously should be tighter than for other jobs. In fact, you should realize that you are starting a path for the person that could lead to a higher position within your company. Some of the ideas presented here may seem unnecessary for individual contributors or low-level leaders, but remember this position may put the candidate in a spotlight where future contributions are judged by other executives in the company. So why not make this a thorough, definitive process and get as many positive attributes as you can? The quality and predictability of the leadership candidates will be greatly improved.

This chapter is one of the longest in the book, but the subject matter is crucial. Picking the right people to be future leaders in your company is one of the most important things you will do. If you mess up a sales call and lose a customer, that will hurt. But choosing someone for a leadership position who bombs out can be catastrophic. I have seen poorly placed leaders run off good employees, create poor morale, and leave very messy HR issues when they eventually leave the company. So placing some focus on looking for the right qualities early in the process will pay off now and into the long-term future.

How many people ever admit that they are not a candidate for a leadership position, that they would not be good as a leader of people? Probably very few. Since popular belief leads us to think that the only way to more money and power is to manage people, and to grow that fiefdom larger, just about everyone feels they can be great leaders if just given the chance. But there are many who are not good at being closely involved in people-to-people situations. This chapter will attempt to give a few thoughts about making the tough calls and bringing only the best candidates into leadership positions.

One of the first considerations in looking for managers is to decide whether to promote from within or to seek someone from outside the team or even from outside the company. There are pros and cons to each.

Promoting from within the team:

Pros

- company knowledge
- business and systems knowledge
- existing team experience and knowledge

Cons

- jealousy from other team members
- Can the new manager lead those who were once his peers?
- Did upper management take the easy way out and pick someone convenient?

Usually, promoting from within the group works well if either of two conditions exists. First, the job is so technical that most of the work the leader will do will be to direct that technical work and it would be impossible to find someone outside the group who knows those details well enough to lead. Or, second, that you have someone within the team who is so good that he becomes the logical choice to lead the team. Never promote someone who you have doubts about because they either expect the promotion or they threaten to quit if they don't get it. Have the hard discussion with them and talk about how you see their best contributions being made. If there are reasons you don't see them as a people leader, be open and honest and tell them. If they do quit, there's nothing else you could have done... move on.

Here are a couple of real examples when this didn't work. A senior sales rep thought he should have had the last two promotions to district manager. He stormed into the general manager's office (three levels above him) and, over two hours, proceeded to present all the reasons of how he supposedly had earned the promotion. The GM relented (possibly just to get rid of him) and gave him the job. What the GM hadn't checked was that the other sales team members hated this guy; they saw him as a kiss-up with a mediocre sales record of his own. Within six months, sales for the team were lagging and a very good rep had quit, so the GM had to remove him and put him in the marketing group. Plus, an intangible, but real, additional loss? A lot of customer good will. This disaster made the Titanic seem like a toy boat sinking in the bathtub.

Another example came about when a VP was promoted to SVP, another VP moved up into her old spot, and they needed to choose a replacement for the VP. This was primarily a sales management position and it was widely expected by the troops that someone with some reasonable experience with actual customers would be selected. The choice was made to promote an operations guy, who had seldom been in front of a real customer. This was the easy way out; he was already in the office and a long-time employee, thus the upper execs had little formal training to do in the ways of the company. He was a nice guy, willing to learn the job, but the learning curve was steep. The troops always liked him, but they saw him of no value to help them get better and to improve sales results. They were very disappointed by the lost opportunity; sales continued on a poor trajectory and some good reps left the company.

Promoting from within the company but outside the team:

Pros

- company knowledge
- reduced concern among team members about the boss' pet getting the job
- often, a bigger pool of talent to choose from
- cross-pollination of ideas within the company
- can be a chance for company executives to make a consensus move

Cons

- possible concerns from within the group about future opportunities for themselves
- new leader may have to learn the team's business
- some possible concern about how well you know the new leader (is his former group in the company dumping their trash on you?)

This option often works well if there is no clear choice within the work team. But, like above, this person must be seen to have been very good at his previous job and have some knowledge of the operations of the new team. It is also important that he was chosen on the basis of both this excellent performance and the likelihood that he can pick up any needed skills for the new position in a short time. And he must have the charisma and communication skills to reduce any tension that might result from the team members thinking that one must come from outside the team to get promoted.

Promoting from outside the company:

Pros

- fresh ideas
- biggest pool of talent to choose from
- Can more closely match experience of the candidate with what you need

Cons

- larger resentment potential by team members
- exact desired relevant experience match will be difficult, if from a different industry
- unless highly recommended by someone you trust, how well do you know the candidate? You could be buying a pig in a poke.

If you decide you need to find your leader from outside your company, here are a few suggestions. First of all, a subchoice....do you want your candidate to come from a competitor, so that he may at least know the industry, or are you looking for some new talent regardless of experience? (This is sort of like drafting a good general athlete rather than a specific position player.)

I suggest you consider building your team, whenever possible, with a mix of these tactics. It is good to have a couple of good sub-leaders who come from the competition, as it is foolish to think your company has all the answers in your particular industry. And hiring some "good athletes" who may not have the exact experience you are looking for but are eminently trainable is good to keep the team growing and learning.

Always trying to promote from within, unless you just cannot do it, as it shows your team members that they can grow within the company, and this tactic keeps good talent on board. There is nothing more frustrating than seeing good talent walk out the door and contributing to your competitor, but it feels pretty good when someone comes to your team from the other guys and becomes an outstanding player.

When considering talent from outside the company, take a look at the résumé closely. The most important item is how many jobs and how much time spent at each one. I remember looking at a résumé with a former boss and hearing the comment, "Look at all the great and varied experience this guy has." My comment back was, "He changes jobs about every two years. What makes you think he will be here longer than that?" Is this person a "job hopper" or a "competition hopper," going from company to company in the same industry, trying to trade some immediate hits for a little extra money? While almost no one stays at one employer for life anymore, a frequent job hopper leaves his current employer for any of several reasons:

- He is unable to cope with problems that arise and leaves at the first sign of difficulty.
- He is "elephant hunting," looking for the big kill of his career so that he can make the big bucks quickly, rather than building a career in an ordered manner.
- He has trouble getting along with others and being a team player.

On the other hand, he may be extremely talented and keeps getting recruited away, but if you think that, do you have any degree of certainty that he will not be recruited away from you?

Be sure to ask lots of questions that are answered to your satisfaction about why he leaves an employer after short stints.

What do you look for in hiring a people leader?

Loyalty. Does this person appear to be the type of good follower (even leaders must be followers), such that he will give a little of himself for the good of the team? Ask questions about how hard it is to change allegiances (even within the company, a person will have to change allegiances among various teams), why that might occur, and how it affects him. While everyone says they "want an opportunity," judge the sincerity of the responses, especially those about why he wants this job and your company.

People-centered. As mentioned previously, everyone thinks they are good at working with others, but many aren't. For a leader, this is crucial, so ask questions about his greatest accomplishments and greatest failures in working with subordinates and peers. Do you think this person genuinely likes people? Do they consider leadership to be an opportunity for their own further advancement or a responsibility for both the team and for mission accomplishment? Ask about what motivates him and look for an answer that involves helping other people to be successful.

Integrity. This is very difficult to judge in a first interview, but ask yourself if you would make a major purchase from this person. Would you let him watch your wallet while you stepped away for a few minutes? Do they seem real and genuine? Are his answers to your questions superficial or deep-rooted? Ask about a time they had to go above and beyond for a customer (internal or external customer), and then the same question about a peer and subordinate. Ask about experience with and how they would handle some difficult people situations, such as absenteeism, suspected theft, lying, and poor performance. Does this person have the courage to confront and handle the tough people-issues in an up-front and efficient manner, all the while acting with compassion and concern? Or will they gloss over the tough issues and allow them to fester?

Knowledge of business. No doubt about it, your subordinate leaders must know the job and have the appropriate skills. A major error in hiring leaders is that upper management assumes that the leader is above all the petty details and just needs to see the big picture only. As mentioned earlier, the leader need not know all the details like the line employees, but must have a good understanding of exactly what upstream groups supply to his team and what downstream groups expect from his team. A good leader need not know all the nuts and bolts of every job within his team, but should know which nuts need tightening and when. You must ensure that the future leader knows this or you are certain that he can and will learn it promptly.

A good example of violating this principle occurred a lot during the electricity deregulation in Texas. Since there was not a lot of experience in this new industry, it was assumed by many that since the telecom industry had recently been deregulated, those folks were interchangeable into the electricity business. This worked well in some cases early on, as many people were learning the new stuff, but even after five years of experience in electricity deregulation, some companies were still importing telecom people and bringing them in at VP levels and above. Imagine the agony for employees in having to teach these new officers some very basic concepts, such as the difference between a kilowatt and a kilowatt-hour. For some quick studies, the learning curve was bearable, but for many others, it caused inefficiency and lost opportunities within the companies. If similar industry talent is reasonably available, your new leader must be something really special for you to pull him from a totally different business.

Well-rounded and grounded. As indicated in earlier discussions, the higher up the ladder you are hiring for, the more of the generalist you are seeking. You seek somebody who knows about a lot of things, with many interests and accomplishments. There is a sliding scale on this requirement—for example, someone to lead an information technology or some other highly technical group might have a lot more direct experience only in that area than you need for other teams. On the other hand, a sales team leader should probably be the most rounded, for his ability to show salespeople how to talk to customers, and he must have the ability to handle the special temperament that comes with salespeople.

So what is "well-rounded and grounded"? I consider someone well-rounded if they can be at home in both a five-star restaurant with linen napkins and a barbecue joint with a roll of paper towels on the table. Try to conduct at least one interview over a meal, and, like Yogi Berra supposedly said, "You can observe a lot by just watching." Someone who can talk about sports and cooking...maybe not expertly in either, but he knows at least a little about them. Someone who keeps up with all the news and can talk about politics (can name his congressman and knows what the Fed is) and the stock market. And, of course, they keep up with the news of your industry. For example, in the electricity business, an important bit might be the current price of natural gas. In any business, they should be able to name at least one of your competitors. Ask questions like this during the interview. And I think a person is grounded if, as mentioned previously, they don't take themselves too seriously. Are they willing to accept constructive criticism? Do they seem to share the values of your company? Can they laugh at themselves? Can they admit mistakes and apologize to subordinates if needed? You'd be surprised at the number of leaders who will never admit a mistake to team members; hiring people like this is a recipe for disaster.

Enthusiastic and motivating. Admit it: someone interviewing with you is like a sales call; you are buying and the interviewee is selling. My advice to salespeople is that you will always be invited back if the buyer enjoys the call and learns something. Did you enjoy talking to your new prospective leader? Did he jazz you up a bit and teach you something? Did he have a real presence, an aura that separated him from others? Were you inspired by the interview? These are some almost intangible qualities that all leaders must possess and you need to try to discover them in the interviews.

Other thoughts on qualities needed for leadership:

Your subordinate leader must be able to see the big picture as well as the details of his group. In effect, the lower-level leaders are the links between the strategic and tactical viewpoints for the company. This leader must have enough of a working knowledge of the company's macro issues to understand, and to be able to communicate to his team, how the team's mission contributes to those strategic goals. The leader who can only focus on his team's mission often becomes too parochial over it and usually does not cooperate well with his peers in other groups. It is important for the leader to know general trends in the industry as well as outside factors that influence the business and the industry, such as weather, general economic conditions, trade issues, commodity prices, etc.

Good leaders also have a variable time outlook. They are comfortable with and efficient at both long-term and short-term vision. The need for both is obvious: the short-term is the accomplishment of the team's mission and, ultimately, making money for the company; the long-term vision will give the leader some foresight to look to the future on ways to improve his team and will help him to know what to ask upper management for to adapt his team to changing conditions. For example, changing customer tastes, regulatory changes, and new technology are all areas that prescient business leaders should watch carefully. Legendary investor guru Peter Lynch built Fidelity Magellan into the world's largest mutual fund at that time partly by watching the stores his teenage daughter frequented in the shopping mall. We should all be so observant...and become so rich!

You seek a leader with a mature outlook as to personal growth and rewards and who will trust upper management to help manage his career. The important factor here is an understanding that the growth of your leader is intimately tied to the success he shows in the job for which he is to be hired. The leadership position you are filling should not be viewed by the candidates as a "stepping stone" to another position. The expectations should be clear that there is no automatic promotion and that future considerations are dependent on how well goals for this position are met over the long haul.

But what if there is a bigger opportunity immediately down the road for this new leader? You are planning to grow the business quickly or have foreknowledge of a higher need in the near future. Should you let the candidate in on your thoughts? Usually, I think the answer is no. You can explain, in general terms, some of the needs the company might face in the upcoming time frame. But you should refrain from saying things like, "If you do well, we will have bigger opportunities for you" or "After a year or so, we could move you up" because this sets a clear expectation in the mind of the candidate from which you may not be able to escape if needed. Many things can transpire over a few months and this prospective leader might not work out even in the current job role. If the candidate possesses the proper amount of maturity, he will understand his role, work hard to meet and surpass goals, and become the obvious choice for future advancement. Did you ever meet some young employee who expects a promotion so often? I remember an arrogant coworker who once told everybody that if he didn't get promoted every two years, then something wasn't right. With those expectations, he would be CEO in just a few years. Let me just say that he did not become CEO, nor get close. Also, it is best not to give "title promotions." By that, I mean that buying off someone's ego and greed with some made-up title without really changing their responsibilities gives them a sense of entitlement that is detrimental to overall performance and morale. In addition, it drives your HR people crazy. Everyone needs to understand that when a position becomes available (either by attrition, growth, or realignment) and you are the logical person for the job (due to performance, skill, ability, and leadership demonstration), you will get your promotion.

A good leader is confident in his abilities and work ethic, and does not become obsessed with concern about promotion. It is the responsibility of upper management to spot these good leaders and to keep an eye on their careers. And the key for upper management here is that they display confidence in their subordinate leaders. No, this is not a job-for-life regardless of performance, but your subordinate leaders should know that they need not sweat the small stuff—that as long as they make good decisions, display a good example for their teams, and achieve good results, their job is not in jeopardy. Be sure your subordinate leaders know that you are immune to politicking and bias in any form, so don't even try it. In fact, everyone should know that you view these things as examples of very poor leadership. This will permit them enough self-confidence to be a strong leader and to not be a politician.

Speaking of work ethic, the good leader has a "smart" work ethic. First of all, be accessible to your people, even in non-work hours. If someone has a problem, they should know that you will at least listen. People usually have loyalty to other people, not to institutions, and trying to be there for your team is the best way to inspire personal loyalty. It is said in the Army that soldiers will not storm a hill with machine guns raining down on them for the flag or the country; they do it for their buddies in the unit and because they know their leaders are doing all they can to keep them alive. A good example of this came from the early days of the recent war in Iraq. An embedded reporter was on patrol with a group of Marines. They were ambushed and three Marines pulled the reporter out of danger. The reporter was quite shaken by the incident and told the Marines that he would give them each five minutes on his satellite phone to call home. The three looked at each other and one told the reporter that their sergeant's wife had just had a baby and he hadn't been able to contact her yet, and could they each donate their time on the satellite phone to him? I remember the reporter retelling the incident, looking into the camera and asking, "Where do we get people like this?" Would it take an incident like this for your team to think this much of you? Or maybe by just being there for them, just a little, might make a world of difference.

Sometimes, people will use your accessibility as a chance for slacking or brown-nosing; the leader will know when to reduce time with certain abusers of the open-door policy. The good leader does not necessarily put in the longest hours on the job, but does not use his leadership position to sham during the work day just because he can get away with it. Leadership, like any important job, will probably need more than forty hours per week, but it should not regularly require sixty hours; that would cause burnout in anyone. You can do those sixty hours occasionally in a pinch, but long-term long hours like that implies a poorly designed work model. Also, a smart work ethic means focusing on the important issues. Don't get wrapped up in office politics or other time wasters, but if these are causing work issues, get involved and solve it.

I remember when coming in as leader of a new group, I discovered the employees in two armed camps, separated by age, lifestyle issues, and petty jealousies. The subordinate leaders accepted this as an immutable fact and worked around it. But I saw that critical information sharing was not happening and I needed to fix it. I remember talking to one person and suggested she get some help from another with a similar issue and hearing her reply, "Well, I don't talk to her." The problems within that team were improved by a lot of individual counseling to let them see that they would all be more successful if they worked together. Also, I would pose problems for them to solve where they would have to work together, even for just a short while. These brief exposures reduced the tension between the groups and efficiency improved significantly.

Finally, a good leader will separate the problem from the person. Have you ever worked for somebody where it was well-known that you didn't want to be the person to deliver bad news? The team should feel comfortable in bringing any legitimate problem forward and feel confident that the leader can help with the solution and that he will not shoot the messenger.

By far, the biggest thing you are looking for in a leader is the ability to **communicate**. When previously mentioning the citizens' perceptions of good American presidents, it was easy to think of two who were perceived to be among the best: Franklin Roosevelt and Ronald Reagan. Why were they more popular and thought of as better leaders than most other presidents? I think it was largely because of their extraordinary ability to communicate with the American people. Whether you liked their policies or not, it is well-accepted that those two men were considered to be among the best at presenting their ideas to the people. There is nothing more important than honest, open, effective, and sincere idea exchanges, both oral and written. By idea "exchanges," I mean they must be two-way, as the ability and willingness to **listen** to others is an integral part of communicating.

Both the written and oral parts are relatively easy to judge if you take a few minutes to think about what the prospective leader says and writes. First, on the written part, you can look at emails, but the only problem here is that it is becoming widely acceptable to use shortcuts, abbreviations, and overall poor grammar in electronic messaging. Also, emails are rarely well-thought out anymore; generally, people just punch out some words and hit 'send' with little, if any, reflection on what they just sent. Search for more formal written correspondence and if you can't find any, ask the candidate to send you a presentation of some sort. One of the most common errors many people commit is improper word choice, such as confusing "lose" and "loose," "effect" and "affect," "to" and "too," etc. A couple of important things to ask yourself when reading a sample, are (1) Was the writing and argument compelling? Does it convincingly make the case the writer is proposing? (2) Was it easy-to-read, appropriately descriptive, and able to hold your attention? Not everyone is a Hemingway, but you don't want to put someone in a position of leadership who might be ridiculed by his team members and possibly embarrass your company. I have suggested business communications classes at local junior colleges for some that need a little extra polish on their writing skills. But the biggest problem with all written communication is that the intended tone of the message is often muted and there is no interchange of ideas; you just read what was written.

As for oral, face-to-face communicating, this is critical for the leader to master. Haven't we all seen those who send emails to co-workers who sit fifteen feet away? Just get up and talk in person! (It's good exercise as well.) A good communications exchange means that defensive walls are broken down and a real connection exists, *a meeting of the minds*, as it is called in contract law. A good oral conversation can share information, can give direction, and can deepen a relationship. But it can do far more! A give-and-take discussion can *inspire*, which is a key goal of leadership. One of the main points of an effective conversation is to never interrupt (ever!). This is easier said than done, especially in a disciplinary conversation when the subordinate goes off on tangents to either avoid the subject or to shift blame. But the leader shows patience and class by letting the other person talk and by skillfully guiding the conversation back to the desired subject and tone. Another important point is to set an example of communicating up and down the chain of command. The leader shows his team that their ideas are credited to them when reported up the chain and that information from upper management is shared with subordinates to the greatest extent possible.

Is it possible to communicate too much? Of course, information that is not ready to be released, or that clearly does not concern the team at the current time, might be withheld until the time is right. The leader should not let on that he is in possession of a secret and should certainly not leak it to a chosen few. Some bits of company information, like executive changes or merger and acquisition information, probably should not be shared with the team unless they are directly involved with the subject. And never repeat gossip or unfavorable information about any fellow employee unless it is critical to the mission. The leader who dabbles in gossip or draws energy from internal company catfights is detrimental to good order and weakens the leadership structure. When the team sees that the leader does not participate in pettiness and anarchy, a major step has been taken in moving from a "boss" to a leader. When approached by a team member who wants to be let in on a confidential matter, use the approach mentioned previously about being able to keep a secret. Future leaders should know that confidentiality is not negotiable; it is an absolute necessity of the job.

Of course, face-to-face conversations may not always be possible, due to distance, time sensitivities, etc., but always spend at least some time with a conversation whenever possible. A phone call is better than an email.

As for the listening skills mentioned earlier, here is a system to reinforce good habits to show that you listen well:

- **Listen thoroughly**; do not multitask when you should be listening.
- Try to **absorb** the words as well as the tone and body language.
- **Cogitate** on what you heard and observed; a few seconds of thought, also known as a "pregnant pause," is okay.
- Then **speak**, trying to respond by repeating back some of the exact words you heard previously; this proves that you were listening and the other person will appreciate it a lot.

What do you look for in how a leader dresses? One key is to expect to be attired at the "upper average" or better, when appropriate. For salespersons, I always advocate one step above the customer so as not to overwhelm the customer or to embarrass yourself. In other words, if the customer is expected to wear jeans, the salesperson wears cotton-type pants (ladies can convert appropriately). If the customer wears golf shirts, the salesperson wears a dress shirt. If the customer wears a tie, the salesperson should wear a suit. A similar spirit might be considered for leaders in an office environment. The leader should avoid dressing below his team. This might be difficult now that many companies have "dress-down" days when jeans or other casual clothing is permitted. I once had a boss who wore jeans on casual Friday; one time they were even ratty, with holes—he looked like the rag man's poor brother. If the leader chooses to participate, the clothing should always be classy and sharp. And if the company has logo clothing that is permitted to be worn at work, the leader should wear that when possible. It shows camaraderie and company loyalty without dressing down. The way to try to be one of the people is by communicating, not dressing to be like everyone else.

Consider the relationship you want the leader to have with the team. As mentioned, being "one of the guys" to some extent is okay. This is best accomplished by not being aloof and by being a great communicator. But there does need to be some clear, even if subtle, separation so that subordinates cannot use a relationship that is too close to gain advantage for themselves or to shirk responsibilities that might lead to mission endangerment. There are two slightly different military examples of this. Consider the relationship between enlisted soldiers and officers in the British and American Armies. Perhaps a vestige from the systems of lords and serfs, the British Army has had a stricter separation, even if unofficial, in which officers and enlisted soldiers generally don't eat or socialize together. Once, while on assignment in Germany, a couple of sergeants in my unit invited me to have a beer with them as their guest in the British NCO club. When the British NCOs saw me there, they couldn't throw me out, but I think they wanted to. They made it very clear they would never invite their officers to have a beer with them. And the British mess halls had separate dining areas for the officers. While it is not a detriment to their fighting ability, it is different and not as effective as in the United States Army, in my opinion. In the US, our society is somewhat less class restrictive and it is much more common to see people from lower economic situations earning themselves officer commissions. In general, the officer population is more evenly spread across demographic strata in the US Army. While there is some social separation between officers and enlisted soldiers, and there are clear rules against fraternization, there are many more examples of interaction and socialization than in the British case. This makes it easier to see that leaders are indeed a part of the team. While everyone plays a different position on the team, the leader is an integral member, separated by responsibility.

Most new leaders often face the seemingly insolvable dichotomy of trying to be liked or respected. Many fall into the trap of being so close to some team members, being best buddies, that it becomes difficult to exercise their disciplinary duties when necessary. Always strive to be respected first. It is critical that the team respects the leader for his position and for his abilities. While we neither salute the leader nor put him on some type of pedestal, having and exercising *personal power* will lead to respect. Using and relying only on *position power* is a recipe for disaster. In my experience, most leaders who earn the respect of their team first will soon be liked by most of them.

Mentioned earlier was the concept of leaders wearing company-logo attire when appropriate. Along those same lines, do you want (or expect) leaders in your organization to be cheerleaders for the company? I think the answer is "yes" in most respects. There is a limit, of course; when there is something blatantly wrong, the leader should acknowledge the facts and not gloss over them. But, in general, all leaders should feel obligated to promote the company and the mission to their team members. While recognizing company challenges, the leader can pump up employees in a realistic way that may not seem hokey or staged. A good attitude to encourage is one of "we're all in this foxhole together." You can always put difficulties in the best light and be a positive source of energy as an example to others.

Do you think George Washington walked among his troops at Valley Forge reminding them about how cold it was and how his British-made blankets were probably warmer than theirs? Probably not. I would think he used the same blankets, told them about how they would all make it through the cold winter, and, come spring time, they were going to whip some British behinds.

A bad example of leadership occurred in recent years when my vice president not only refused to buy our company's product for his home use, but bragged to others that he was buying a competitor's product at a cheaper price. I think he did this so as to say, "Look how smart I am." Believe me, at his level of compensation, the price difference was a pittance. Behind closed doors I discussed this with him several times, pleading with him to not advertise this disloyalty, but he didn't see any problem with what he was doing. Here was the case of someone promoted to his position because of his brains, but he never would give that small amount of himself to the team and to the concepts for which we stood—and that makes one of the greatest differences between a boss and a leader.

CHAPTER 6

SELECTION CRITERIA FOR GOOD
TEAM PLAYERS

Whether you choose team members from within the company or industry or from elsewhere, the criteria you might use are not as critical as for potential leaders, but there are some similarities. While you may not be looking for a leader-in-training, some of these criteria ideas may improve your team overall. Sometimes, you're just looking for worker bees, not queens. In any case, it is good practice in interviewing job candidates to ask questions in an attempt to ascertain whether some of the qualities listed below are evident prior to making the hiring decision. And you never know when you might come across a really good potential chief, so keep your options open when you interview.

Always remember that anyone interviewing for a job is likely to be nervous, and this might affect how they respond to your questions. Do whatever you can to put the candidate at ease so you can discover the real person. Try some non-traditional things, like walking around the building while you talk.

Here are some thoughts for choosing team players:

Long-term personal growth. As with leaders, the "flash in the pan" might make an immediate impact, but someone who realizes that the best way to get rich quickly is to get rich slowly makes for a good team member. They are content to learn and hone their craft for a certain period of time. While they need to be shown opportunity and potential, they understand that they must prove themselves before expecting advancement. The time period for expectations of advancement and superior performance might be shorter for some candidates than others, but you should look for some evidence of patience and maturity. Questions like, "When might you see yourself making a significant impact at this company?" and a very open-ended request like, "Tell me about what you expect to achieve in the first few months here" might help to give you some measurable points in this area.

Loyalty. Ask interview questions like, "What are important values to you?" "If hired, what is your obligation to the company?" "Can your loyalty be bought?" All legal questions, and the answers, tone, and body language might help you to ascertain this quality of loyalty. As mentioned in the Introduction to this book, loyalty to a company is often seen as a rare quality today, but you should expect at least some. You are still hoping to find and inspire whatever loyalty you might be able to generate later, even it is only to you as a leader.

Team spirit. Is this person someone you'd like to work with? A co-worker with a sense of optimism, someone easy to talk to, a cooperative and willing contributor is the goal of every hiring manager. Ask about the greatest contribution this person has ever made to a team. "What was your best and worst team experience?" "Have you ever been a team leader?" "Describe a perfect team situation." Answers to these questions might give you a sense of their team spirit and whether the candidate is willing to give a bit of himself to be a real team member.

Communication skills. As with leaders, although to a lesser extent, this quality is important for most jobs. You might consider asking the candidate to make a presentation, maybe in front of a couple of other team members, as part of the interview process. Ask questions like, "Describe your most difficult communication experience." Listen carefully for complete, well-focused answers to your questions. If at all possible, try to get some evidence of written communication proficiency, perhaps a little deeper than email traffic.

In searching for the right team members, I often am reminded of my greatest shortcoming, that being a lack of patience. It is hard to accept sometimes, but there are two employee growth areas in which the leader must be patient. Competence and experience usually take new employees some time to master. Of course, you say, experience takes time. But I'm talking about *creating* experience by aggressively going out and finding job information, not waiting for it to happen and then claiming a certain amount of time experience. Would you rather hire someone with two years of *aggressive* experience or someone with ten years of *passive* experience? But the two areas in which the leader should never have to show patience are strong effort and a good attitude. If the members continually exhibit these two qualities, they will likely achieve competence and experience more quickly and more deeply than others. From day one of each team member's employment, the leader should exemplify effort and attitude.

Choose every team member carefully and don't be in a hurry. Although these selections may not become future leaders, and in some cases you may be only looking for individual performers, there is nothing wrong with honing your interviewing skills to more effectively search for those who might one day lead your company.

CHAPTER 7

A Leader's Use of Data

Winston Churchill is supposed to have said, "There are three types of untruths: lies, damnable lies, and statistics." It is well known that numbers can often be twisted to support almost any opinion and it is certainly true that too many numbers are expensive, unmanageable, and misleading. The time and resources it takes to assemble them can cause your company to miss many opportunities.

Good leaders use data to support their positions, never to be the position itself. Data does not drive decisions; it gives meaning and is some measure of veracity to directions that leaders determine need to be taken. For example, leaders are concerned about sales and competitive trends and decide that a new product needs to be introduced. Data, on customer preference and similar information, can be collected and analyzed to determine the extent and depth of the opportunity. The good leader is on top of his business and uses data to support his thinking. If the information comes back and does not confirm the leader's position, then it is time to rethink the issue. But launching ever-lasting information campaigns is costly and inconclusive. Never throw a bunch of spaghetti on the wall and see what sticks….that wastes a lot of good spaghetti. Rather, periodically pick out a few strands of spaghetti that you think are done and throw *them* on the wall. In doing this, if you can't amass a decent batting average in picking out the good opportunities, you might consider doing something else for a living.

At first glance, you may think this chapter deals only with high-level strategic decisions. True, some of these principles can be used for decisions with very large implications, but most any workplace decisions can be guided by these suggestions. For example, employee incentive programs, customer presentations, and workplace physical improvements are just a few of the limitless applications of this concept of getting just enough data to support the best decisions, then moving forward.

One of the main suppositions of this book is that good leaders are in the forefront of the ideas and the people. All other supporting functions can be done under the appropriate leadership level. One of the worst examples of leadership involved a VP who ran his life on numbers. He was poor at eye contact and, even worse, simply could not connect with people on a personal level. All decisions were driven by data, and then only after lengthy and laborious discussions with the chosen few, those he let in on the process. You can imagine the frustration of being responsible for a certain part of the business and not getting any input into the decision. This guy spent his entire day poring over sales and marketing reports, eschewing all other sources of information, especially just *talking* with people who were doing the work. Probably his biggest mistake was in creating new pricing schemes without talking to either the sales team or any customers. He got to know the numbers well, but never acquired a *feeling* for the business. Obviously, he didn't last too long.

A leader with a good feel for the business should trust his judgment and experience and make appropriate decisions based on many factors, with data being just one. Also, he should trust the people he has put in place to do the work. If too much time is spent on things like, "We just need one more market survey" and such, it can lead to the famous "paralysis by analysis" in which the feeling is that you can't get enough data. History is replete with examples of failure caused by over-analysis. Consider Union General McClellan during the peninsula campaign of 1862. It was evident that he held considerable advantages over the Confederates in terms of men and supplies. Yet he was way too cautious, believing reports on the enemy to be far larger than reported by scouts and wasting so much time that the enemy was able to prepare to counter any thrust McClellan made. Most military historians agree that the Civil War would have ended three years earlier if McClellan had exercised very reasonable risks by attacking his way all the way into Richmond.

On the other hand, one of the business world's most famous flops might have been caused by not getting enough data before the decisions were made. Some of you may remember the "New Coke" of the 1980's. The most popular soft drink in the world was scrapped for a much different taste and left hordes of devoted customers howling. Very soon thereafter, the old Coke came back. A little more market surveying might have prevented this fiasco. At least that's the official version and this could be a good example of not getting enough data to support a big decision. As a side note, I offer a different opinion. In the Introduction to this book, I mention an executive from Coca-Cola as an exemplar of great leadership. I think the entire New Coke episode might have been a well-planned and brilliant marketing strategy. The free publicity generated by this event was staggering and priceless. It seemed like every media outlet in the world was working this story about the millions of heartbroken old Coke aficionados. After the very public apology and restoration of the old Coke formulation, the company emerged with an even stronger market position and retained its loyal consumer base. A most interesting chain of events whatever the intentions, but it still illustrates the point of attaining sufficient data to support major decisions.

Get the right amount of data to confirm your thinking; if the data doesn't support your thinking, then you might collect more, but be prepared and willing to change your mind if the data is significantly counter to your thoughts. At some reasonable point, action is required. All businesses need timely decisions. We all have seen opportunities lost because of leaders trying to make the decision so obvious and foolproof with boat loads of data that the boat sank without leaving the dock. If you're trying to collect so much information that the data clearly points to the decision, you are not taking advantage of the supposed business knowledge of you and your team...the costs of this extra studying is outlined later in this chapter.

People who spend more time with numbers than with people, and trust numbers more than people, should not be leaders of people. One of the few of those to admit he was not a good leader was a chemist I worked with quite a bit. He was a very good technical chemist and was credited with many patents for our company. As is so often the case, the way to reward him for good work was to make him a group leader. The move did not work and after a short period of time, he requested to be taken out of the leadership role. He realized that he was happiest doing his experiments and crunching the numbers. Not many will admit something like this because conventional wisdom says that the only way up is to become a manager of people. But putting the wrong people in these positions usually ends much worse than this example, as the person will have to be removed from the leader role. A better method is to authorize senior positions with some authority measures for those not eligible to be people leaders.

Here are a few keys to a leader's effective use of data in decision-making:

1. Use only as much detail as necessary. Continuously slicing and dicing seldom gives a clearer picture and wastes money and time. Ask yourself if that extra decimal place on the data will really improve the decision.

2. Lump categories together as much as possible unless a point needs to be made within a specific area. For example, if it is decided that a shade of blue is desired for a new product, you could try to get consumer tests on a hundred different subtle shades. By the time you finish, consumer tastes could turn to red. Pick a few good shades of blue, do some testing, and move.

3. Use an appropriate time frame for collecting and analyzing all your numbers. Often, too short of a time frame is used to make decisions on very slow-moving trends. At a former company, we would have a major presentation every month on sales, profitability, products sold, competitive behavior, etc. Three employees would spend almost all their time collecting, sorting, analyzing, and building a "deck" for the data for this report. It was all done very professionally, and gave some good insight into our business. The only problem was that the business moved too slowly for the monthly frequency of this big report. Everyone agreed that it was imprudent to make any big decisions based on one month's trends. We would have been much better off if we had done the full report quarterly with maybe some monthly brief updates. Our staff could have been better deployed and the frequent requests for information from our sales staff would have been fewer so they could

have spent more time selling. So why did we continue with the monthly grand presentations? Because a change would have required the leadership to get out of their comfort zone. It would have left a hole in their calendars, which might make them feel guilty for not exercising some real leadership. Of all the resources your team needs, the only one you cannot get more of is time. After a while, people will tire of the seemingly constant fire drills that lead to fifty-five-plus-hour workweeks that don't result in any real progress. Use their time in productive ways that lead to meaningful progress towards unit goals. That makes work fun and profitable for all.

4. Spend the appropriate amount of time and resources gathering data. Not all end results are equal; some major initiatives always deserve at least some time and effort, but you must know how much time to spend when smaller issues are evident. It is demoralizing to the team to spend way too much time on seemingly trivial points. If smaller issues need more attention, be sure to communicate why to the team, as best you can.

5. Decide when added detail on your project becomes counterproductive. At some point, the costs and time delays of data collection and analysis becomes asymptotic (see illustration below). A leader who is versed in the industry, understands the project, and is decisive will know when the data supports the project and when to start implementing. Additional data beyond the critical point seldom makes the decision more obvious. Often, it confuses the decision process by opening far too many options and it is always costly. Again, does that extra decimal place improve the decision?

6. Spread around the burden of data-gathering and analysis. Some leaders feel they are too good for this "grunt work" and just want to see the results. But by taking a piece of the

project, even a small one, the good leader learns several things. First, the time and labor required in data acquisition is better understood and appreciated. Second, the leader can ensure that the project is aimed in the right direction so that it can be completed with a minimum of resource dedication and cost. There are no unpleasant surprises along the way that require redo. The most inefficient leaders play "bring me a rock" with their team members. Here's how that monstrous game works: the leader says, "Bring me a rock." The employee, being conscientious and dedicated, searches hard, thinks he has the perfect rock, and sets it on the boss' desk with a touch of pride. The boss then says, "I want a smaller rock." Again, the employee searches long and hard and comes back with a smaller rock. The boss says, "Too small." The employee then brings in a perfectly sized rock; the boss then says, "I want a round rock." The cycle repeats itself over and over with the colors and shapes of rocks. The boss (certainly not a leader, in this case) does this, first of all, *because he can.* Other reasons for such behavior is a lack of understanding on exactly what he wants, but he is afraid to admit that to the team. That boss is waiting to see the perfect result so that he will know what it is. The leader should have enough vision to know the strategic direction needed. By participating in the data project and giving some parts to as many employees as reasonable, the leader gets maximum input and buy-in, while also keeping close enough to the work to keep it on track.

7. Have a good understanding of the true costs of data-gathering. I once asked the president of one company and the COO of another the same two questions: "When you arrive at a meeting and somebody slaps a twenty-five-page, full-color PowerPoint down in front of you, do you ever consider the amount of man-hours and the opportunity costs of that deck?" And: "At the end of that hour meeting, when everyone is scrambling away

so they can attend yet another meeting, you see that only the first four pages of that deck have been discussed. Do you ever feel guilty about that?" Those two questions made me about as popular as a skunk at a picnic, but both the officers got my point. The clear point is that the existing system served them and that satisfied them. But in a well-run company, the officers serve the system—they mold it not to satisfy themselves, but to achieve goals and to build a successful team and a profitable company.

One of the most difficult parts of good leadership is to make decisions, sell them to the team, and make the initiative successful when you have imperfect information about the issue. For example, in introducing a new product to a certain marketplace, it is easy to feel that you will never have enough information about the new market or the competition to go forward with selling it. Or you may have to consider layoffs or staff additions. Whatever the issue, you know you must take a calculated business risk and launch the initiative. At some point, you need to have confidence in the information that you have, declare it sufficient, and use your experience and drive to make a good decision and move forward (or not). Continued study can be costly in many ways. Consider the graph below:

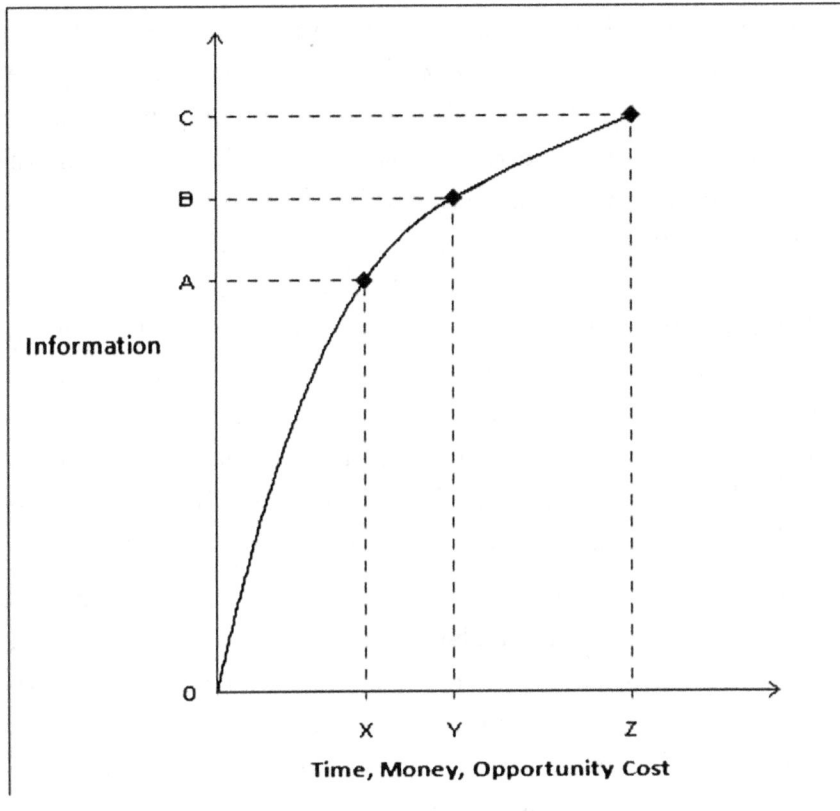

A lot of information about a subject can generally be obtained fairly quickly and easily. For example, if you're considering launching a new product, your own knowledge and the embedded experiences of your team and other resources within your company can probably get you a lot of the needed information. We all know the Internet is a wealth of information as well. Talking to some trusted and valuable current customers about product needs will make them feel an even closer part of your work family. And you're a consumer, too, right? Would *you* buy this new product? If you want to build a new facility, many of the points above will work, in addition to tons of information from the local area Chamber-type organizations, other property owners near your proposed location, and local publications should be scanned. In short, a great deal of low-cost, easily obtainable, high-quality, high-impact information is out there...go get it!

Consider this amount of information as Point A on the vertical axis of the graph. Without a large investment in time and money, and at a reasonable level of total cost (Point X on the horizontal axis), you will have a great deal of information necessary to make the decisions. Even if it is felt that additional information is needed, the leader can extend the information-gathering to Point B at a fairly even exchange for opportunity cost at Point Y. But, above that, danger can befall those who fiddle while Rome burns. All along, the good leader is considering the information acquired and whether it is sufficient to make the decision and move forward.

Note that the information curve is asymptotic, that it flattens out so that *perfect information can never be obtained.* Want to throw more spaghetti against the wall? That means there is that much less to eat! Many people do not believe this; they continue to pour resources into a black hole, getting decreasing marginal amounts of *useful* data. You can always get more information about any subject, but is it useful—does it make a material difference in the quality and profitability of the decision? One boss of mine was poring over reams of minutiae and made the comment, "Gee, this is interesting." She was correct; it was interesting. But it was also so granular, and applied to such a small part of the issue, that it was effectively unusable. And the resources that it took to get that level of detail were expensive and created inefficiency.

And you must consider one other very important point. If you see this issue to be important to your business, you must assume your competitors see it, also. Maybe they haven't, but the more time you spend on the decision process, the more likely a competitor will scoop you. This opportunity cost can be the most devastating consequence of too much detail.

The key is to avoid over-studying a decision point.

Once, my employer had decided to expand into a new geographic area. Some early studies were done about the market opportunity, and mainly because so many of our competitors were starting business there, our company made the announcement that we were soon to enter that market, along with a new brand name to be used there. Then began the amazing grind of bureaucracy and mismanagement. The leaders were so afraid of making a mistake (mostly of making themselves look bad) that studies were repeated *ad infinitum,* more internal teams that only had a small stake in the new market were brought into the decision process, and decision timelines were delayed on a routine basis. In short, the decision process totally broke down because of the inability of the leadership to use their experiences and their knowledge about the business to take reasonable business risks. They wouldn't even kill the project because of the negative publicity (and the expectant bad personal hits they might take), so they decided to study it forever. Here are some of the bad things that happened in this case:

- So many employees had put so much time and effort into this project that morale was negatively affected by the delays and the seeming lack of commitment to the project by leadership.

Doing the same work over and over (so that management could view it as "current") is also demoralizing.

- During the delay, competitors continued to solidify their footholds in that area, making our entrance there even more difficult, as we would have to dislodge them. The window of opportunity was closing fast.

- Good faith was lost with potential customers. The announcement had been made; there was the expectation that the company would begin selling and it didn't happen. Never give customers less than what they expect.

- Perhaps most important, this mindset made the leadership lose faith in itself, although they would not admit it. When I drew the graph above on my boss' whiteboard, he said, "You have to understand. We need to be careful because we've been burned before." Pretty self-defeating attitude, isn't it? It was as if he had said, "We know we make bad decisions so we have to second-guess ourselves." And that attitude, like rumors among the ranks, becomes infectious to the point where the employees lose faith in the leadership. So instead of being on the team with Alexander the Great, we found ourselves working for Alexander the Mediocre. I doubt anyone would want to wear a T shirt with that on it.

After making the decision, the next part is to make an effective "sale" of this to your team. A key part of this is to make them part of the information and process prior to the decision. Perhaps some of the information-gathering needs to be done in secret due to marketing plans or whatever. Consider an example of a potential company merger with a competitor. While the plan cannot be discussed openly, there are probably parts of this information step that can be asked of your team, even if in a generic way (for example, open-ended questions like, "What do you think about our competitors?" and "How should we position ourselves vis-à-vis our competitors?"). Their responses might be valuable as the merger is negotiated in secret. Then, when the merger is announced, the leader can remind the team members that they were part of the process. It now becomes partly *their* decision and they will likely run with it and embrace it more than if they think it was forced down on them. This exact scenario was executed well by upper management in a merger that I was part of in the chemical business.

Assure them that any "holes" in analysis are covered. Assure them that the opportunity outweighs the risks. And be sure to tell them that the companies that are most successful excel in mastering the art of calculated risk-taking.

Some years ago, my team was presented with a limited-time opportunity to help some customers arbitrage between natural gas and electricity pricing. It was our idea, and by teaching the customers how to do it, we could earn some significant consulting fees while the customers achieved huge savings. This was something no one had ever done before, yet it presented few identifiable risks. Since the window of opportunity would only last a few months, I knew we had to move quickly. In my talks with our division senior vice president, he asked me who could give ultimate permission for us to do this. My response to him was, "If we continue to ask permission, someone will eventually say 'no.'" At that point, the idea is either dead or will take so long to implement that the window will close on you. This SVP (who became a mentor of great leadership to me) approved it, and the idea worked well; we made a lot of money in a few months until the opportunity did close due to commodity market pricing. Had we analyzed this deal for just a few weeks more, we would have made nothing. If you have the ability to do something, and you have examined and quantified the risks to the appropriate extent possible and found them to be reasonable, then **lead.**

CHAPTER 8

Assessing the Performance of Team Members

An open, fair, and honest performance assessment is critical to good leadership for several reasons, some listed below. Too often, a performance appraisal is seen as a requirement and drudgery by management, rather than the opportunity it is to totally clear the air and openly and frankly discuss how well someone does their job. So, what are some reasons to do a good appraisal?

1. It is important in selecting people for future promotions to leadership positions. The appraisal can be shared with others in future selection processes to give a clearer picture of the candidate's potential.

2. It serves as a valuable tool to weed out those who are not performing at standard. There is nothing more frustrating than needing to pare down the work force and not having any good reasons to keep or let go of certain employees. Also, a documented record of substandard performance is the key to meeting HR criteria to ensure that the release is done correctly.

3. A thorough review is important to providing feedback to reinforce desired behaviors. By memorializing good performance in written form during the review, the employee is more likely to respond favorably by continuing those actions.

4. It is good for team morale and improves overall team performance. Too often, people feel they get rated by a "black box," and management sometimes reinforces that belief with slipshod reviews that are not timely nor are reflective of actual performance and events. It helps to make the playing field seem level to all participants and that they are all judged fairly.

What does a leader need to conduct outstanding performance reviews?

The first and most important trait needed is **courage.** Could the Cowardly Lion conduct a good review? Probably better than some managers do. The key is to not be afraid that the employee won't like you if you say something negative or make suggestions for improvement. Remember, your job is to be fair and get the mission accomplished; if the team likes you, that is just gravy. If you accurately and fairly point out the good and the bad in a review, the employee will most likely respect your thoroughness and intellect, even if they are angry and don't want to believe the truth.

Being **organized and efficient** is another important factor in performance appraisal. A good way to manage the information for an appraisal is to not try to get it all together at the last minute. It is difficult and not fair to try to remember all the good and bad stuff that may have occurred over a long period of time in a short time prior to the review. You may be influenced by more recent events and will not give full weight to some things that happened earlier in the appraisal period. A good way to keep up with this is to keep a record of events as they happen. Old-school guys like me will keep a file folder on each employee in a locked desk drawer. Of course, this can be done in a data base as well; just make sure it is private and secure. Each time something memorable happens (good *or* bad—don't only do it for bad things), write a brief note, with the date, on a card or slip of paper and put it in the appropriate file. A couple of days before you start to write the appraisal, spend some time reviewing your notes so you can be accurate with these examples in the write-up. Obviously, if the event is substantial, don't wait for the review to mention it to the employee. Good or bad, talk to them and try to either reinforce good behavior or correct bad behavior quickly. And remember to praise publicly and criticize privately.

Gathering the information for a review is an important step. Remember I earlier quoted that noted leader Yogi Berra, "You can observe a lot by just watching." You need to observe behavior and results so they can be noted.

It goes without saying that you must **know your team.** One way to do it is management by walking around. Your schedule may not permit a lot of this but every leader should make a habit of cruising the workplaces whenever possible, talking to the team, and asking questions about their jobs and what they need to do to be more successful. Even a few minutes of this will pay large dividends. This makes judging the cold facts more meaningful and removes the favoritism accusation of, "I got a bad review because the boss doesn't even know me." During these visits, try to evaluate the employees' responsiveness, enthusiasm, and skills. Take into account personal situations like shyness and intimidation, remembering that a lot of folks may feel like they're in the spotlight when the boss is visiting. I have found in sales situations that sometimes those who are not doing a good job at putting up numbers have career days when I travel with them to visit customers. So what are they doing on days when I'm not with them? Ask candid questions about their perception of the company, the mission, team performance, and their role on the team. Sometimes, how they answer those questions is just as important as what the answers are. Try to judge if the employee embraces unit goals and norms.

A subject that is part of performance appraisals, as well it should be, is **compensation**. Insecure leaders often dance around the topic. One former boss of mine could not look you in the eye while discussing money. I assure you, it is an important topic to your subordinate; you should be confident, straightforward, and secure in the position you are taking on their comp package. Give *them* the credit for good news if you're giving them a raise instead of trying to ingratiate yourself to them by stealing the credit. If you're getting a good raise or promotion, would you rather hear your boss say, "I fought to get this for you" or "Congratulations, you've earned this"? On the other hand, if the news is bad, such as in a very small or no raise, don't apologize or kick upper management around. Be totally up front with something like, "As you probably know, business is tough right now and we all need to bear through this and help to improve the bottom line." In the case of poor performance leading to no raise, again say the truth and put yourself in the potential solution, perhaps, "We need to improve your job performance before you get a raise. Here is a plan that we can do to try to get you there."

These tips, with that large helping of the aforementioned courage to be upfront and honest, should help you to conduct effective, fair, and accurate performance assessments. It is one of the most critical jobs of the leader.

CHAPTER 9

The Rewards and Benefits of Good Leadership

No doubt, companies can excel with effective leadership. Sometimes, the company can have a product and business situation that is so compelling that not even poor leadership can kill it for a long time. A good example might be General Motors. Many people instinctively bought their products out of a strong brand loyalty or because of family legacies and other reasons. The company was in a long swan dive for many years due to successive poor leadership, and lack of foresight killed the company to the point where GM had to accept a government bailout just to barely survive. Because of their previous market dominance, GM had such a long way to fall, and lots of market share was gradually erased over many years before the final fall. And, indeed, brand dominance has been at least partly responsible for GM to recently reclaim its number one market position. But few companies are in that situation; most businesses fight it out in highly competitive arenas, and good leadership is often the difference between success and failure on a fairly short-term basis. At the top, a group of team-playing, good-communicating executives is critical. And in mid-management ranks, those who can direct people towards unit goals are no less important. Check out the record of General Electric as to how a "brick-and-mortar," old-school manufacturing company can prosper because of great leadership throughout the ranks.

What does a good display of leadership mean to that individual? More money? Quicker promotion? More power? Maybe. But the real benefit goes back to something mentioned earlier, and that is the attainment of **respect** from subordinates, peers, and superiors. The subordinates respect working for you because you help them to get better, breed a culture of success, and are fair. The peers want to emulate your success and will seek your advice on leadership issues. And your superiors are appreciative for your performance, for the few people-problems brought upwards, and are probably congratulating themselves for giving you the chance to lead. Gaining respect seems to be a habit with many people; you can see respected business leaders carrying this over into all parts of their lives. I've seen this in Little League board meetings and various other non-business areas.

Remember the difference between respect and fear. There is an old axiom (not really true) that says a healthy fear of the boss is a good thing. But think about that for a minute. Isn't having an employee respect the boss a much better emotion than fear? Being fearful strongly implies that an employee is not really happy and will dump this job as soon as he can for another one that does not make him fearful. Going back to our definition of leadership, will the employee enthusiastically give his full measure of ability to someone he is afraid of? I am reminded of a sales manager that I had the displeasure to work with as a peer. His style was slash and burn—people were disposable. If a salesperson didn't meet their quota over the short term, they first turned into trash in the manager's view and then were quickly disposed of. The culture in the group was one of fear. A handful of salespeople realized that one of the only ways to survive was to become great politicians, feeding the manager's ego (unfortunately, this often worked). As you might imagine, this manager had a fairly good two-year record—in other words, he was moderately successful for two years at several different companies. I think that some managers build a tenement of fear because it is easier than building a cathedral of respect. Respect lasts a lot longer than fear. And I would argue that being respected is a better feeling than being feared. And very often, respect can lead to affection, your people will like you, at least those whose opinions you value.

Good leaders should be moved around the company whenever possible. Their imitable qualities are infectious and can shore up flagging morale and performance in many places where needed. Also, it can show upper management if this good display of leadership can be replicated or maybe if it was just a flash in the pan. Varied assignments can give the good leader more rounding and is a good test as to the potential for senior positions. If the leader has earned respect and accomplished goals in a small group, a natural reward is to give him a bigger opportunity. When people do a great job of digging, give them a bigger shovel!

A corporate culture that inspires good leadership is essential. First, a good compensation system will reward team play, at least partially. I believe that almost every employee should have some variable pay based on how well they cooperate with others to get the job done. Many say this is impossible to measure, but that sentiment is often a cop-out by managers afraid to do their jobs. As mentioned previously, a good leader spends time with his team and knows the contributions of each member. More importantly, they are not afraid to have the hard conversations when needed.

Earlier, we discussed "management by walking around" and I think it should apply to all leaders, but with limits. A former employer of mine had a brief policy in place that commanded various vice presidents to go visit different business units. So my VP of sales would spend a day going to a production unit just to walk around. Nobody knew him at the plant, nor cared that he was there (what could he possibly do to make them better?), but he was getting his check in the box and some frequent flyer miles, too. But there were no requirements for him to walk around his own areas of responsibility. Wouldn't it have been better if he spent that time in his own business unit? Even the CEO (if it weren't for his picture on company literature on the walls, nobody would have known his face) could spend some time in the work units. Think about this as a great icebreaker: a C-level executive approaches a worker in his chain of command and introduces himself by saying, "Hi, I'm the Easter Bunny but with smaller ears." Seem a little hokey? People respond to that type of folksiness since it shows a lack of pretension and some non-threatening humor.

The executives at one of my companies had a pretty bad history of decision-making. The rank and file came to despise and ridicule them because they didn't even know them at all. The wall between C-level and employee became impermeable because, as the company situation got worse, I think the suits were afraid to talk to their people except in carefully choreographed, all-employee meetings in which questions from the employees were seeded to trusted shills. This made an even deeper hole because no matter what the executives proposed in the future, the employees would not give the idea any initial backing. I think that if the executives had come out of their cocoon a little more informally, more employees would have given them the benefit of the doubt and at least supported some of the ideas a little more strongly.

The company culture should also inspire open communication. Certainly there are projects and confidential information that cannot be disclosed to all employees. But consider the example of Enron, where executive leaders were telling their employees to keep buying company stock when the big guys were dumping theirs. The principle remains to be as open as you can and never, never lie to your subordinates. Often, I've had to tell someone, "Sorry, I just can't tell you any more right now, but I will catch you up as soon as possible." The point is that people want to hear the news from as high a level in their chain of command as possible rather than rely on water-cooler rumors. Of course, the higher-level leaders have so many people to touch and more limited time, yet they can try.

We discussed "management by walking around" but also consider "lunch and learns," where team members can hear it from you in an informal ambience. If you can't have the food brought in, then don't feel bad about having the group bring their own, sort of a "brown-bag lunch and learn." If you make the effort, the team will appreciate it. But be careful not to overload the communication angle. Immediate supervisors meet with their teams and keep them in the loop as much as possible on a first-line basis. But as the level of the leader increases, the frequency and specificity of information communicated must diminish. Team members should see their direct manager more frequently than they see upper-level management. Never permit the situation where higher level leaders see your team more often than you do.

Good leadership is often the defining cause of good corporate performance. It is worth significant efforts to field the best leaders, with the best training, and the best backing possible.

CONCLUSION

This book cannot make you something that you cannot be. Let's face it: there are some people who cannot be good leaders. They may find a political way to get to a leadership position, but they do poorly at it, and, as mentioned in the Introduction, their team members will never refer to them as great leaders. But if you do have a sense of comfort in your own skin, a true desire to make your team better, and you get your primary satisfaction from the accomplishments of others rather than from your own accomplishments, then perhaps a few tips from this book can make you an even better leader.

Becoming a good leader is a process; it never ends. Care about your people. Care about the mission. Keep practicing, keep rehearsing, and keep communicating.

ABOUT THE AUTHOR

A native of Houston, Texas, David Ciarella graduated from the University of Texas at Austin and then served four years active duty as an officer in the US Army. He has since accumulated almost thirty years of experience in sales and sales leadership positions in the chemical and power industries.

For more information on leadership topics, please see topnotchleadership.com.

www.ingramcontent.com/pod-product-compliance
Lightning Source LLC
Chambersburg PA
CBHW051343170526
45166CB00002B/931